TWAYNE'S WORLD AUTHORS SERIES
A Survey of the World's Literature

Sylvia E. Bowman, Indiana University
GENERAL EDITOR

FRANCE

Maxwell A. Smith, Guerry Professor of French, Emeritus
The University of Chattanooga
Former Visiting Professor in Modern Languages
The Florida State University
EDITOR

André Chénier

TWAS 418

André Chénier

ANDRÉ CHÉNIER

By RICHARD A. SMERNOFF
State University of New York, Oswego

TWAYNE PUBLISHERS
A DIVISION OF G. K. HALL & CO., BOSTON

Library of Congress Cataloging in Publication Data

Smernoff, Richard A
  André Chénier.

  (Twayne's world authors series ; TWAS 418 :
France)
  Bibliography: p. 159 - 64.
  Includes index.
  1. Chénier, André Marie, 1762-1794. 2. Authors,
French — 18th century — Biography.
PQ1965.S6   841'.5   76-50038
ISBN 0-8057-6258-2

To Laura and Peter

Contents

About the Author

A native of Holyoke, Massachusetts, Richard A. Smernoff received his B.A. from Yale University, the Certificat from the Sorbonne, and the Ph.D. from Princeton University. He is currently Chairman of the Department of French, Italian, and Classics at the State University of New York at Oswego. Before coming to S.U.N.Y., Dr. Smernoff held a teaching position at Smith College. While working on his doctoral dissertation, he was the recipient of a Woodrow Wilson Dissertation Grant and later received a State University of New York Research Grant.

Professor Smernoff has taught courses not only in eighteenth-century French literature, but also courses in Existentialism, the woman in the French novel, and the absurd in twentieth-century literature. His publications include articles on Aragon and Laclos.

Preface

I have written this study in the belief that André Chénier stands as one of the supreme interpreters of his age. His life span of thirty-one and a half years pales when compared to Voltaire's eighty-four, and the Pléiade edition of his collected works is dwarfed by the latter's voluminous output. Chénier is nonetheless a central figure, not because he was a poet in an age allegedly indifferent to poetry or because of the spectacular circumstances of his death, but because his writings represent an eloquent and profound statement on the questions raised by the Quarrel of the Ancients and the Moderns of the previous century. His work touches on all categories of living, to borrow a phrase from Diderot — the aesthetic, political, moral, social, and religious — yet his contribution is not limited to the realm of the history of ideas. Chénier's writings embody the very multiplicity of the eighteenth century and reveal a man who was neither Neoclassical nor Preromantic or even alternately the one and the other. For Chénier sought to accommodate order and feeling, the primary passions, technology, and spirit of the universal with the independence of the new.

For various reasons André Chénier's work had a long history of neglect. First, there are biographical factors to be considered. Chénier's having published only two poems during his lifetime is itself not a singular phenomenon — the history of belles-lettres is filled with the names of artists for whom recognition came posthumously — but in Chénier's case the dramatic events surrounding his death raised his person to the ranks of legendary status and paradoxically condemned him to greater obscurity. At the time the first collection of his poems was brought out by Latouche in 1819, he was more known for his death than his life. As Chénier's manuscripts came before the nineteenth century public (it was not until 1899 that the last of the poet's manuscripts were permitted to be read in the

Bibliothèque Nationale in Paris), scholarly inaccuracies were passed on from one edition to the next by editors who were interested specifically in elevating Chénier to the ranks of a precursor of Romanticism.

A second obstacle to an appreciation of Chénier's work can be traced to interpretations of the Enlightenment that prevailed for generations, namely, the view of the eighteenth century with regard to the allegedly polar and therefore irreconcilable qualities of Voltaire and Rousseau, representing Neoclassicism and Preromanticism respectively. The twentieth century has done much to revise this simplistic approach to eighteenth century France. More than forty years ago Ira Wade stressed the importance of diversity among Enlightenment thinkers, whereas Peter Gay has more recently shown the eighteenth century *philosophes* as far from utopian in their understanding of the role of reason in human history.[1] The notion that the Age of Reason saw deterrents to the concept of a model society everywhere has been accompanied by the studies of Saisselin, Finch, and Kopf, among others, which have pointed to the fact that neither poetry nor poetics became extinct during the Enlightenment if one judges from the sheer quantity of poems and treatises being written.[2]

Although recent criticism has asserted that eighteenth century literature should not be approached exclusively as a function of philosophic ideas, a rigid historiosity still persists. Paul Dimoff, who devoted his life to Chénier scholarship, and to whom all students of Chénier must be grateful, nevertheless pointedly entitled his 1936 two volume work *La Vie et l'oeuvre d'André Chénier des origines jusqu'à la révolution française*.[3] Dimoff attempted to justify his decision not to pursue Chénier's life and work beyond 1790 because of his belief that Chénier had "two existences, the one literary and the other political."[4] Dimoff went on to state: ". . . the epicurean yields to the man of duty; the man of letters vanishes before the citizen."[5] What is implicit in Dimoff's thesis is the belief that Chénier's works motivated by political factors, those which belong to what the twentieth century has labelled "littérature engagée" (loosely translated as the "literature of commitment"), are somehow less worthy of being classified as literature than the earlier poems modeled on the ancients. Dimoff's assessment of Chénier's work in terms of what he considered a marked dichotomy between literature and politics has a twofold implication. It ignores the fact that during the Revolution

Chénier synthesized his thoughts on such matters as love, friendship, society, and human destiny, all of which he had treated before 1790. In addition, Dimoff's preoccupation with Chénier's sources and intellectual formation has the effect of treating from the perspective of the history of ideas what Dimoff characterizes as pure literature and therefore seems to give credence to the idea that eighteenth century literature must be approached as literary history.

Clifton Cherpack has attacked the notion of the historical approach to eighteenth century French literature but Pierre Chartier's more recent statement represents the prevailing view: "More than any other, the literary history of the eighteenth century assumes the form of a history of ideas."[6]

In my study of Chénier I have been guided by the belief that no artist's work can be separated from his milieu and private fortunes. At the same time I have attempted whenever possible to show the literary qualities of Chénier's poetry. In response to Dimoff's thesis concerning Chénier's two existences, I contend that the poet and the political analyst became as one during the Revolution, that Chénier's writings became increasingly influenced by his concerns as a moralist, and that he achieved the fullest expression of his belief in art as a universal phenomenon and in the artist as a moral legislator who must chronicle his times at precisely the period when his own life became inextricably linked with specific revolutionary events.

After briefly discussing Chénier's life I treat his poetics, followed by chapters on the bucolics and elegies. A chapter on the Revolution is followed by a concluding chapter on the last poems. Limitations of space have prevented my treating Chénier's epic poems in this study. Although Chénier himself believed that his reputation would be based on "L'Hermès," "L'Amérique," and "Susanne," it becomes increasingly evident that these three works will be of interest principally to Chénier scholars as historical pieces.

Dimoff's three volume edition of Chénier's works and Walter's Pléiade edition are the two principal primary sources I have consulted. References to specific pages of these work have been indicated in the text following each quotation. Numerous quotations from Chénier's works have been given in both the original and my own English translations in order to present specific illustrations of Chénier's use of language.

I wish to express my deep appreciation of Professor Maxwell A. Smith, French editor of *Twayne's World Authors Series,* for his painstaking and generous assistance in the preparation of this book. His incisive comments have been extremely useful to me.

This study has been undertaken in the hope of providing an integral picture of Chénier that will lead to a greater understanding of both his work and the vitality of the Enlightenment.

Chronology

1762   Birth of André Chénier in Constantinople.

1765   The Chénier family leaves Constantinople; André is placed with his father's sister and brother-in-law, the Bérauds, in Carcassonne; his mother and siblings go to Paris and his father settles in Morocco.

1767   Louis Chénier is named Consul in Morocco.

1773   André joins his mother in Paris and meets the painter Cazes in her salon; enters the Collège de Navarre where he makes several lifelong friends, including the Trudaine brothers, the de Pange brothers, and Abel de Malartic de Fondat.

1775   Makes his first trip to the Trudaines' Château de Montinguy.

1778   First examples of his writings in verse, an adaptation from Homer and an imitation of Virgil's eighth Eclogue.

1781   Completes his studies at Navarre; makes commentaries on Malherbe's poetry and meets frequently with Le Brun and the Marquis de Brazais to discuss poetry; falls in love with a dancer whom he designates as Lycoris in his poetry.

1782   Joins an infantry regiment in Strasbourg as a cadet; sees the Marquis de Brazais briefly while in military service.

1783   Louis Chénier retires and joins his family in Paris; André leaves Strasbourg in March. Has attacks of kidney stones; makes a visit to the dungeon of Vincennes; conceives of writing his elegies and bucolics; probably begins work on both "L'Hermès" and "L'Amérique"; works on "L'Aveugle."

1784   Is advised to go to mountainous region because of his health; travels to Switzerland with the Trudaines between September and November.

1785   Meets Mme de Bonneuil shortly after returning from Switzerland; this encounter inspires the poems which bear the inscription D'z.n. and Camille. In the same year he begins his liaison with Marie Cosway.

1786   Is introduced to the painter David by the Trudaines; travels to Italy with the Trudaines; writes Italian elegies; probably begins work on "La République des Lettres" by the end of this year.

1787   Friendship with Alfieri; first meeting with François Lecoulteux, the "Fanny" of his odes; breaks with Mme de Bonneuil; departs for London in December in order to serve as secretary at the French Embassy in London; writes "La Liberté" and "Hymne à la justice."

1788   Works at the embassy in London; reads English authors such as Arthur Young, Pope, and Milton; does research on the English Constitution; writes marine idylls.

1789   Growing disenchantment with life in England; lines written in Hood's Tavern; the Revolution begins in France with the Tennis Court Oath and the storming of the Bastille; Chénier returns to Paris in the summer. In August his brother Marie-Joseph's play *Charles IX* is presented at what would later be known as the Odéon. A few days later André returns to London.

1790   Returns to Paris, probably in June; Civil Constitution of the Clergy is formulated; uprising of the Swiss at Châteauvieux in August; writes "Avis au peuple français sur ses véritables ennemis," marking his inauguration into political journalism; is a member of Société de 1789, which later became Feuillant Party; returns to London in November.

1791   Returns permanently to Paris; begins writing for *Le Moniteur* and later for the *Journal de Paris;* publishes in June one of the two poems he saw in print during his lifetime, "Ode au Jeu de Paume."

1792   Writes numerous articles for the *Journal de Paris;* publishes "Hymne aux Suisses de Châteauvieux"; is forced to go into hiding during the summer; Tuileries invaded in August; monarchy abolished in September; his exact whereabouts during last months of year not known; spent time in Rouen, Le Havre, and Paris.

1793   Louis XVI executed in January; Revolutionary Tribunal created on March 10; Marat assassinated in July.

Chronology

1794   Is arrested in Passy on March 7 while visiting the Marquis de Pastoret; is taken to Saint-Lazare. Hears of the Duchesse de Fleury, Aimée de Coigny, and writes "La Jeune Captive"; writes last *iambes;* is brought before Revolutionary Tribunal on July 25 and is guillotined on same day; Robespierre falls from power on July 27.

1795   Death of André Chénier's father.

1801   Marie-Joseph Chénier publishes "La Jeune Tarentine" in March under the title "Elégie dans le goût ancien."

1819   Hyacinthe de Latouche publishes the first collection of André Chénier's poems.

1862   Becq de Fouquières publishes the *Oeuvres poétiques* of André Chénier.

1962   Exposition in the Bibliothèque Nationale de Paris commemorating the bicentenary of André Chénier's birth.

CHAPTER 1

The Life and Times of André Chénier

A MAJOR thread of Albert Camus' *L'Etranger* is that any man's life appears elusive if looked on from the outside. The apparent simplicity of André Chénier's life is deceptive, for Chénier pursued with singleminded zeal his goal of being the modern Homer. His life can be divided into six periods which reflect not only geographical changes but shifting worldly experiences:

1. Childhood in Constantinople and Carcassonne (1752 - 1773).
2. Paris: The Collège de Navarre; worldly society, friendships, and love (1773 - 1782).
3. Military Service in Strasbourg (1782 - 1783).
4. Travels in Switzerland and Italy; liaisons with Mme de Bonneuil and Marie Cosway (1783 - 1786).
5. London: The French Embassy (1787 - 1790).
6. The Revolution; Fanny Lecoulteux (1790 - 1794).

Externally, his life followed a well-defined pattern. Except for the Strasbourg and London periods when his daily life was filled with nonartistic tasks, he attempted to perfect the craft of poetry, and thus fulfill his life's ambition. At the same time, he was far from being the type of artistic recluse that Flaubert and Proust have come to embody. Because of his amorous temperament and capacity for friendship, his recognition of the need for self-discipline was often in sharp conflict with his primary drives. His vitality, however, was a function of the very tensions which this duality produced. A figure of the late Enlightenment whose first writings date from 1778, the year in which both Voltaire and Rousseau died, he knew Paris salon society and such figures as the painter Louis David without being a part of the philosophic party or of the group that launched the *Encyclopédie*. Destined to remain poor among wealthy aristocratic friends, he never showed the signs of Jean-Jacques Rousseau's acerbic misanthropy, even when his feelings of solitude in London

17

became overwhelming. Physically unattractive, he nonetheless enjoyed the company of some of Europe's most fascinating women. A passionate admirer of Hellenic civilization who lived his life without ever setting foot on Greek soil, he was, at the same time, a man of the eighteenth century who aspired to identify and preserve the moral values that were common to all great civilizations.

I *Childhood*

The few documents that relate to André Chénier's childhood reveal that he was born on October 30, 1762, in Constantinople. Both his father, Louis Chénier, and his mother, Elisabeth Lomaca Chénier, were of middle-class backgrounds. Louis Chénier had left his native France many years before André's birth in the hope of improving his fortune. A man of scholarly temperament who published in the 1780's a three volume work on the history of the Moors, and who, although having spent very little time with André, was a source of encouragement to his son's artistic ambitions, Louis Chénier was never able to provide adequately for his family of four sons and one daughter. Because of his father's financial circumstances André was forced at the age of three, in 1765, to live in Carcassonne with his father's prosperous sister and brother-in-law, the childless Bérauds, while his father went to Morocco and his mother went to Paris with his siblings.

It was by his mother that André Chénier was first exposed to Greek culture. The Lomacas' ethnic origins have been the subject of controversy — whether they were Catalans, Italians, or Levantines has never been conclusively proven — but what is essential for our purposes is that Elisabeth Chénier believed she was of Greek descent and had Greek songs and dances performed in her household while her children were very young. It is highly improbable that the intricacies of Greek culture could have been grasped by André Chénier by the age of three. Far more logical is the assumption that his awareness of his Hellenic ancestry became conceptualized when he was reunited with his mother in Paris after 1773, a period when Elisabeth was known as "la belle Grecque" and kept a salon known for its exotic Oriental flavor.

André Chénier's childhood seems to have passed without incident. From every indication he suffered no traumatic effects from having been separated from his immediate family. A passage describing his childhood, written in the 1780's, suggests that he was a sensitive, carefree youngster, endowed with a vivid imagination, who took pleasure in imitating the actions of adults whom he had observed: "When I was still a child I would make beautiful chapels . . . I ferreted everywhere to get hold of a few small pieces of satin . . . in order to make a beautiful chasuble of gilded paper. I chanted the mass. I preached. I was listened to, people made the sign of the cross . . ." (*Essai sur les causes et les effets de la perfection et de la décadence des lettres et des arts,* Pléiade, p. 634).

If any single trait that emerged during André Chénier's first eleven years influenced his adulthood, it was his love of independence. Undoubtedly, his separation from his parents at the age of three resulted in a greater measure of self-reliance and an appreciation of family and friends. These two qualities served him well when, in the depths of despair in London, he ultimately rejected suicide by recalling the affection and love he could count on from so many people. It was this vaunted independence, associated in his mind with the ancients' precept of self-knowledge and self-mastery, that would lead him to proclaim that the artist alone can judge his work. Because he believed so strongly in the sanctity of the artist's own judgment, he wished to avoid public criticism of his work and, with the exception of two works commemorating revolutionary events, refrained from publishing his poetry.

II   *The Paris Years*

One might well imagine that André Chénier's move to Paris in 1773 was an abrupt shock in view of the quiet rustic existence he had known in the South of France. The Paris he came to know was not, however, the teeming capital that, in fictional accounts, corrupts young men from the provinces, but was a vibrant metropolis that could satisfy both his intellectual and emotional needs.

The first was fulfilled when he was enrolled by his father at the celebrated Collège de Navarre, the most progressive lycée in Paris at the time and a school normally reserved for the sons of wealthy aristocrats. Navarre was, therefore, of major importance in Chénier's life, for it not only shaped his intellectual development but provided a social milieu that would later influence his perception of political events.

As a student at Navarre he was exposed to the standard classical authors, including Plato, Aristophanes, Theocritus, Catullus, Lucretius, Virgil, Horace, Tacitus, and Cicero. In addition, he read a wide range of French authors — Pascal, Molière, Corneille, Racine,

Voltaire, Montesquieu, Jean-Jacques Rousseau, Raynal, Condorcet, Mably, Buffon, Le Brun — and the English authors Milton, Shakespeare, and Richardson. His tastes in literature were already well formed. We know, for example, that he greatly admired Malherbe but criticized Ronsard. He was not, moreover, given to uncritical praise of eighteenth century French authors in vogue and had unfavorable words for both Voltaire and Helvétius.

In 1753 the faculty at Navarre had instituted the first class in experimental physics. Chénier keenly felt the spirit of the scientific revolution while at college. The numerous works which reflect his desire to impose new ideas (scientific discoveries and the challenge of uncovering new laws governing the physical universe) on old forms (epistles, idylls, odes) can be traced to his college years, and include such works as the "Epître à Bailly," in which he declared that the poets of his time have not even a smattering of astronomy, of natural history, or of sciences. At Navarre Chénier was confronted with the task of imposing the spirit of the new science and philosophy on poetic forms, a concept that forms the basis for "L'Hermès," "L'Invention," and "L'Amérique." Just before completing his studies at college his poetic vocation seems to have emerged:

> Hardly had I seen sixteen springtimes shine,
> Already liking the peace of a studious refuge,
> Not knowing anyone, unknown, alone, tranquil,
> My humble voice, on one side, attempting some concerts,
> My young muse dared to stammer some verses.[1]

One cannot take seriously his declaration in these lines that he was alone, for it was at Navarre that he was to meet the Trudaine brothers, Louis and François de Pange, and Abel de Fondat, later the Marquis de Malartic. What is noteworthy about these men, particularly the Trudaines, is that their attitude toward Chénier was always one of unwavering, supportive friendship. It was through his college friends, all of whom came from families of greater wealth and prominence than his own, that Chénier was to meet many of the women with whom he fell in love. The great warmth and affection he felt for the Trudaines, François de Pange, the Marquis de Brazais, and Abel de Malartic have come down to us in many odes and epistles.

While a student at Navarre, Chénier was able to spend considerable time in his mother's salon, where he was introduced to such notables as the painter Cazes. His determination to make poetry his life's work seems to have been crystallized during this time, for in "La République des Lettres" he described the sublime pleasures he derived from inviting a few intimate college friends to his private "Louvre" and sharing with them his artistic ambitions. In 1781, the year he left Navarre, he fell in love with a dancer at the Opéra whom he designated as "Lycoris" in a cycle of seven poems. Love in these works is defined principally in terms of the epicurean delights of physical possession as opposed to the brevity of life and love. The Lycoris cycle reveals a poet who was able to rely on his technical skills to invest conventional literary themes with new shadings and harmonies.

During his eight years in Paris, André Chénier acquired an education which, in breadth of curriculum, approximated the Renaissance ideal. In matters of literary criticism he revealed himself as essentially undoctrinaire, as evidenced by his "Commentaire sur Malherbe," written in the late 1770's. The dualities of his personality surfaced now. Enamored of the ancients' simplicity and taste, he was equally attracted to the moderns' spirit of adventure that had led them to uncover new laws governing the universe. Writing in the 1780's of the pleasure he took in retreating to his private abode in order to collect his thoughts and compose, he had a vision of the artist that involved expansion as well as introspection and he did not disdain the diversions of love and friendship that Paris offered. His awareness of the beauty of the past and the vitality of the present formed an integral part of his intellectual and emotional development during these years. These factors combined in his most polemical work, "L'Invention," to produce his theory of *innutrition:* The aspiring poet must think and feel like the ancients but he must not be afraid to forge new trails by incorporating into his work subjects that are the unique reflections of his age.

III   *Strasbourg*

Leaving the Collège de Navarre in 1781, Chénier discovered that his family's precarious financial position created serious obstacles to his desire to be a poet. An artist like Gustave Flaubert, who is cushioned by family wealth, can devote five years to writing *Madame Bovary*. A writer who needs money can work at a feverish pitch and produce manuscripts in record time, in the manner of a Balzac. Or a would-be artist can live the bohemian life and endure the poverty and struggle associated with such an existence. The Chénier family's finances ruled out the Flaubertian mode, André's temperament was incompatible with prolific creativity, and his having known the Trudaines and other aristocrats at a college frequented by the sons of the rich precluded his even considering the third way. A military career seemed the most feasible alternative open to him and he enlisted as a cadet under a new recruitment plan which promised to bring him a commission in a short time. In August, 1782, he joined the Angoumois Regiment, garrisoned at Strasbourg.

Chénier found military life almost entirely displeasing. Strasbourg, with a population of nearly fifty thousand, was a prosperous city in the eighteenth century because of its commerce and industry. Thanks to the presence of numerous civil and military functionaries it boasted an active social life. Yet, the rigors of military training and the fact that he had to share his room with three other cadets made Chénier's adjustment to life in Strasbourg very difficult. His failure to receive the expected commission, moreover, increased his disillusionment. His one consolation during his life as a cadet seems to have been his friendship with the Marquis de Brazais, a captain in his regiment who, as an absentee officer, visited Strasbourg infrequently. Chénier's dislike of the military life is clearly shown in an epistle in which he speaks of the Marquis de Brazais' absence: "Les ruisseaux et les bois et Vénus et l'étude/Adoucissent un peu ma triste solitude" ("The brooks and the forest and love and study/Soften somewhat my melancholy solitude" [Dimoff, vol. 3, p. 187]). In short, the period of less than a year that he spent at Strasbourg was one of frustration for André Chénier. Separated from his friends and from the stimulation of Paris he wrote epistles to his friends. These months were more than a mere hiatus in his career, for he left Strasbourg more determined than ever to dedicate himself to writing. Scarfe's observation that the Strasbourg experience turned him into an arch enemy of the Ancien Régime seems unfounded.[2] Quick to recognize injustice, Chénier would, nonetheless, have opposed any political or social movement that threatened to destroy the lifestyle enjoyed by his aristocratic friends.

Finally, it is not unreasonable to assume that his plans for many of his longer works, including "L'Hermès" and "L'Amérique," took shape during this year. He had already been exposed at college to the scientific discoveries of Newton, Bailly, and Buffon, he had enjoyed liaisons with women and had profited from the kindnesses of solicitous and steadfast friends. Strasbourg was a disappointment for

André Chénier but it also marked a year in which he was able to look back on his recent experiences in Paris and dream about a glorious career as a modern Homer.

IV 1783 - 1787: Switzerland, Italy, Mme de Bonneuil, and Marie Cosway

The next four years of André Chénier's life were among his most productive. Although it is impossible to date most of his works precisely, notes and references strongly suggest that from the time of his departure from Strasbourg in 1783 until his arrival in London in 1787, he completed or wrote numerous drafts for bucolics and elegies and wrote substantial portions of "L'Invention" and "La République des Lettres," in addition to collecting material for his epics and the *Essai sur les causes et les effets de la perfection et de la décadence des lettres et des arts.*

After leaving Strasbourg, Chénier went to Paris. His father had retired and was able to be reunited with his family for the first time in many years. Because André now suffered excruciatingly painful kidney stone attacks, he was advised by his doctors to go to Switzerland. As is the case with so many incidents in Chénier's life, it is difficult to determine the exact dates of his travels, but most critics agree, basing their deductions on references in certain poems, that he left for Switzerland in 1784 and Italy in 1786. It is known that in both instances he accompanied the Trudaines and that these brothers paid his expenses. Scarfe has noted how many aspects of the aristocratic life Chénier shared: "A striking feature of Chénier's formation as a poet is its resemblance to the education of the poets of the Renaissance. Though of bourgeois origin he had a noble and classical education, followed by military service, private studies, foreign travel and a post in an embassy."[3]

Both Trudaines and Chénier found the Swiss model of liberty very much to their liking. Switzerland was already very much in vogue among the French, as suggested by their numerous *récits de voyage.* Although Chénier did not write a single poem in which he specifically spoke about his impressions of Switzerland, it is obvious from certain lines in the "Hymne à la justice" of 1787 and from his definition of political models in his writings of the 1790's that he viewed the simple customs, the republican straightforwardness, and the nationalistic pride of Switzerland as the contemporary counterpart of ancient Greece and Rome. The pastoral settings of many of his bucolics can in fact be said to have been influenced by his Swiss travels as well as by readings of the ancients and by Jean-Jacques Rousseau. In short, Switzerland enabled Chénier to enrich precise elements of his pastoral poetry.

Returning from Switzerland he met, in 1785, Mme de Bonneuil, a woman eight years his senior who was married to a rich old man. The nature of her stormy relationship with the poet, characterized by separations and unfaithfulness, was recorded in the cycle of poems bearing inscriptions to D'z.n. and Camille. Love, equated here to a general state of disequilibrium, did not yet provide for him the lyrical inspiration of his days with Fanny Lecoulteux. Only after enduring three years of uncertainty and frustration was he able to effect, in 1787, a final rupture with this woman.

In the meantime, in 1785 he had met Marie Cosway, wife of the celebrated portrait painter. She, like Mme de Bonneuil, was married to a much older man. If Lycoris appealed to Chénier's senses and Mme de Bonneuil to his pride, Marie Cosway can be said to have fit his desire to celebrate the eternally feminine, not the corrupter of men but the creature whose moral virtues are a source of inspiration. The feelings Chénier associated with Marie Cosway were no longer destructive but rather ennobling.

Chénier's 1786 trip to Italy offered an entirely different perspective from that of Switzerland. His interest in Italian language and literature was not only a natural outgrowth of his interest in ancient Greece and Rome, but was also encouraged by his liaison with Marie Cosway, who was born in Florence. Italy, as depicted by Chénier in the works that have come to be known as the Italian elegies, was a haven for the artist: "Je puisse au sein des arts vivre et mourir tranquille!" ("I can live and die tranquil in the bosom of the arts!" [Dimoff, vol. 3, p. 9]). Beyond the spectacle of ancient ruins and the treasures of Italy's museums, he realized during this trip that he had not yet accomplished his life's ambition of immortalizing his century in his poetry as the ancients had immortalized their civilization. As Dimoff has observed:

What he wanted to seek out in Italy and in the Orient was, above all, almost as much as physical health, moral health. . . . With the passing of his youth he regretted all the more how frivolously he had spent it and experienced even more anxiety at the thought that the works on which he had hoped to immortalize his name had not yet taken shape. . . .[4]

Although Chénier was to reap intellectual sustenance in 1786 and 1787 from his meetings with the painter David and the Italian poet

Alfieri, whose ideas influenced the *Essai sur les causes et les effets de la perfection et de la décadence des lettres et des arts*, he, who at the age of twenty-five had never contributed to his own support, was beset by financial problems of mounting proportions. In 1787 he had met Fanny Lecoulteux, who was to inspire in him the most profound veneration he ever felt for a woman. Yet, he was forced to recognize that his artistic ambitions could never be brought to fruition while matters of financial urgency plagued him. It was in the hope of relieving his family's financial miseries that he set forth for London in 1787 in order to work at the French Embassy.

V *London*

André Chénier was no happier in London than he had been in Strasbourg. The fact that his position at the embassy was not commensurate with his talents does not suffice as an explanation for his growing despondency. Nor could his reunions with Marie Cosway in her London salon revive his spirits, despite the fact that the Cosways' musical soirées were a meeting place for some of England's most gifted minds, including Horace Walpole, the Duchess of Devonshire, the Countess of Aylesbury, the Marquis of Townshead, Lord Erskine, Lord Sandys, and Lady Cecelia Johnstone. Chénier's position at the embassy, moreover, left him considerable free time to frequent such London sights as Covent Garden, Drury Lane, and the Haymarket.

Hitherto Chénier had shared his century's Anglomania. Like Montesquieu, he had admired the English system of government and had stated in his "Hymne à la justice," completed just before he left for London, that he hoped to find in his new surroundings a haven where he could live in tranquility. Certainly the English were class-conscious but the French were also, notwithstanding the fact that he was welcomed everywhere by the Trudaines and their associates. Scarfe offers the following interpretation of the growing rancor and despair of Chénier's London writings: "This tendency to feel himself an outcast goes far towards explaining the sense of abandonment and solitude which runs through the *Elégies* and *Iambes*. Chénier's pride and isolation were not derived from Rousseau; they were not romantic, literary qualities but came of his own temperament and social predicament.[5]

As word of Revolutionary events in France reached London, Chénier's concern about the state of affairs in Paris led him to return to the French capital in the summer of 1789. One senses his joy at be-

ing able to leave London and return to Paris, even in such precarious
times.

VI   *The Revolution*

Chénier's life and work from 1790 to 1794 are discussed in detail
in the chapter on the Revolution. Inaugurating his political writings
during the Revolution was the "Avis au peuple français," which appeared in August, 1790. From his thoughts in the *Essai* and other
writings of the 1780's, it is clear that he viewed the artist as a moral
legislator who must define and reveal in his writings the moral
imperatives of his times. His contributions to the *Moniteur* and *Journal de Paris*, as well as his numerous odes and *iambes* inspired by
Revolutionary events, were, therefore, entirely consistent with his
views that the artist cannot detach himself from his political and
social milieu.

Politically, Chénier's voice reflected in these writings the essentially conservative stance of the *philosophes*. Opposing justice,
moderation, and reason to violence and mob rule, he viewed the
Revolution more from the perspective of a moralist and psychologist
than from that of a systematic political analyst. Although he clearly
identified himself with a moderate position which, by implication,
was anti-Jacobin, his independent spirit refused to allow any com-
promise of principles he considered inviolable. To the radical factions of the 1790's he was an enemy of France. To later generations
of historians, who claimed that his having feigned a more radical
position would have saved his life, he was singularly naive.

Becoming increasingly vocal in his insistence that the hope of
Europe in general and France in particular lay in the preservation of
values that had remained unchanged from one civilization to the
next, Chénier revealed in his odes and *iambes* his most intensely
lyrical expression of man's primary passions and concerns, including
love, hate, fear, human nature and destiny, and life's brevity. It was
thus that André Chénier, in the last months of his life, most fully exemplified the principles of naïveté and "inventive imitation" that
formed the core of his poetics. To the destructive impulses of the
Revolution, the event that brought his century to a close and in-
augurated a new age, he opposed the ideals of moderation, measure,
and reason, and in so doing linked his voice to those of antiquity and
of other ages that had exalted man's capacity for idealism rather
than nurturing his potential for animality.

CHAPTER 2

The Poetics

THE *Princeton Encyclopedia of Poetry and Poetics* defines poetics as "a systematic theory or doctrine of poetry."[1]

It is apparent in examining Chénier's work that, unlike the Boileau of the *Art Poétique* or even the Voltaire who commented on Corneille's plays, Chénier never concerned himself with poetics in a systematic way. Even in "L'Invention," the work in which he addressed himself most directly to the problems confronting the aspiring writer of a modern epic, he refrained from treating such questions as style, rhythm, rhyme, and other linguistic devices. On the other hand, his lengthy discussion of his conception of the creative act, his insistence that the work of art cannot be considered independently of its creator, and his belief that literature is comprehensible only when viewed against the background of the society in which it evolved — all three ideas are consistent with his approach to literature from the perspective of a moralist. The five works in which Chénier dealt with aesthetic matters — *Essai sur les causes et les effets de la perfection et de la décadence des lettres et des arts*, "L'Invention," "Epître sur ses ouvrages," "La République des Lettres," and the "Commentaire sur Malherbe" — point to a doctrine of the poet as the supreme interpreter of his age, and are therefore of prime importance not only as documents on Chénier's aesthetics, but, most significantly, as works which show that his revolutionary activity was entirely consistent with his views on literature.

I Essai sur les causes et les effets de la perfection et de la décadence des lettres et des arts

A. *Introduction*

In the striking first sentence of his Introduction — "There is no happiness for any living species, other than following what nature

27

destines to it" — Chénier evokes the famous opening line of Rousseau's *Du Contrat Social*,[2] which has led Kopf to speak of the *Essai* as
a union of classical antiquity with Enlightenment philosophy.[3] As
"the central concept of the age," in Rémy Saisselin's words, nature
could mean all things to all men, and when proliferated in such concepts as natural man, natural rights, natural state, natural innocence,
and natural goodness it tended to obscure rather than clarify: "In
time though, thanks to Rousseau, the eighteenth century came to
know what nature was not: clearly, its opposite was art."[4] A basic
premise of Chénier's *Essai*, however, is the notion that men wanted
to band together in groups early in their development and that this
penchant distinguished them from animals. This theory of man's
socializing instinct is in complete variance with Rousseau's
primitivism, his belief that man could not even begin to concep-
tualize life in social groups. It is essential to note, therefore, that
although Chénier and Rousseau appear to be concerned with the
same questions, their basic premises are different. Because he never
believed that man's having formed social groups was a natural
process, Rousseau attempted in his *Discours*, in Mornet's words, "to
discover what is primitive and therefore legitimate and what is
merely a complication and a perversion."[5] Chénier, on the other
hand, argued that man's desire to live in society with other members
of his species is itself the result of his desire for harmony and
therefore, far from being a perversion, is a desirous state (*Essai*,
Pléiade, p. 621).

Chénier went on to state that the establishment of a system of
ethics based on principles of equity and justice became part of man's
life as a social being, for without such general safeguards disorder
and anarchy would have prevailed. Whereas Rousseau believed that
men are innately good, Chénier, more in keeping with Voltaire,
believed that men can strive toward the attainment of the greater
good through their conscious efforts. Man was therefore an active
agent in Chénier's scheme, a being who was capable of reason, feeling, emotion, and perception. Although he did not embrace the concept of Manichean dualism that characterizes certain of Voltaire's
contes, his rejection of man as a creature consigned to a passive
fatalism and his emphasis on constant evolutionary change made it
clear that he never believed that there existed a time in man's history
when there was absolute uniformity of thought or behavior. Viewing
man's psychological duality, Chénier wrote that some men in the
newly formed society strove for glory and thus attempted to place

themselves in a superior rank over their fellows. On the other hand, the virtuous deeds and the writings of others acted as a normative influence on those who might otherwise have become too self-seeking. Literature, then, according to Chénier was considered a moral palliative. The link between this observation and Chénier's remarks (in such political essays as "Avis au peuple français" and "Les Autels de la peur" during the Revolution) concerning the influence of inflammatory writers shows to what extent he believed that the direction of the Revolution was influenced by written propaganda. In support of his contention that Chénier exaggerated the power of the written word, Scarfe notes that in 1791 Chénier declared that all the good and bad done during the Revolution had been the result of published works.[6]

Literature, in Chénier's scheme, was a natural development of man's socializing instincts, following the existence of an oral tradition of military exploits. The literature of early societies, however, fulfilled in reality a function that was more descriptive than influential, for the breakdown of just institutions was accomplished by the enslavement of art through the influence of patronage. While Chénier regarded writing as a sublime art, he never blinded himself to the dangers to which the artist, under pressure, could often succumb. Here, as in other writings, he upheld his vaunted principle of the artist's independence. As he worked on the *Essai* and witnessed the succession of events that led to the Revolution, Chénier made it clear that independence meant the artist's being able to speak with integrity and clearly did not mean his isolating himself from his environment. At the early stages in the writing of the *Essai* Chénier continued to turn to his select group of friends to nurture his artistic ambitions and, more important, wrote in a spirit of better understanding the state of letters.

One passage from the *Essai* bears quoting at length. It reveals that Chénier's personal involvement in what he considered the deplorable state of the arts and letters of his age led him to embrace the methods of the philosopher, literary historian, and social historian in his determination to show the complexity of the physical, moral, and social causes upon which the literary production of a people depend:

As for me, opening my eyes around me at the end of my childhood, I saw that money and intrigue were almost the only means of achieving anything. I resolved therefore from that point on, without considering if circumstances allowed me, to live always far from all machinations, with my friends, in retreat and in the most complete freedom. Shocked to see letters so prostrated and the human race not thinking of lifting its head, I abandoned myself often to the distractions and wild doings of a strong and impetuous youth; but always dominated by love of poetry, letters, and study, often chagrined and discouraged by fortune and myself, always supported by my friends, I felt at least in me that my poetry and my prose, appreciated or not, would be placed among the ranks of a small number of works that have not been influenced by any contemptible action. Thus, even in the ardor of age and even at moments when bitter necessity interrupted my independence, always taken with these favorite ideas, and, at home, while travelling, along streets, taking walks, reflecting all the time on the perhaps foolish hope of seeing the rebirth of good disciplines and seeking, at the same time, in histories and in the nature of things, *the causes and the effects of the perfection and decline of letters*, I believed that it would be good to condense in a simple and persuasive book the reflections on these matters that the passage of a number of years had ripened in me. (*Essai*, Pléiade, pp. 624 - 625)

Moreover, he believed that his economic and social circumstances would enable him to speak out without being constrained by any form of literary patronage, a stand of impartiality and independence in literary matters which Scarfe sees equally applicable to Chénier's politics.[7]

Here and in other writings Chénier revealed his ability to distinguish between the artist's involvement and leadership in public affairs and the artist's pandering to fashionable social conventions. In a word, Chénier came to view the artist as one who inspires and not as an inspired man who must separate himself from the masses. Margaret Gilman has observed that the eighteenth century "brought Parnassus into the salon," the salon here taken to mean an earthly, human phenomenon rather than a specific eighteenth century institution.[8]

What is original in Chénier, that is, what sets him apart from Montesquieu, Rousseau, and Mme de Staël alike, is his appeal to the artist to be an active force in society by opposing corrupting influences. And so, the Introduction, revealing Chénier's design to act as an ameliorative agent through his simple book, suggests that at the very moment he was describing in detail his penchant to band together with a select group of fellow artists equally dedicated to the task of preserving their artistic integrity by remaining free of society's corrupting influence, he was countering this tendency to retreat by writing an explicitly didactic work. To the extent that

Chénier wished to discuss the relationship between literature and
society, he proposed the following three large headings:
I.   "Causes which favor letters"
II. "Causes which are harmful to letters"
III. "Exhortations and examination of present circumstances"

B.   *"Causes which favor letters"*

1.   *"On laws"*

Chénier's entry on climate consists of only one fragmented line:
"laws, customs, soil, the climate, and the gods, etc. . . . big piece.'
(*Essai*, Pléiade, p. 627). Chapter II, "On Laws," begins on a note no
less dramatic than the Introduction: "Tyranny and democracy are
the only governments where men of obscure birth can achieve the
highest ranks in their work, but by entirely different reasons and
means" (*Essai*, Pléiade, p. 628). Chénier's division of government
into three forms — the despotic, the monarchical, and the
republican, the latter of which is further subdivided into the
aristocratic and democratic — is identical to Montesquieu's divisions
in *De l'esprit des lois*.

Dimoff has noted that Chénier was nearer to Rousseau than
Montesquieu with respect to his ideas on equality and that, like
Rousseau, Chénier thought that good laws would elevate the
character of citizens.[9] It is not surprising that Chénier saw in a
democratic form of government the surest means of attaining an
equitable division of power.

Although in Chénier's view an elected official's position in a
democratic state is never secure, he must appear to possess at least a
semblance of virtue whereas in a monarchy a prince must like those
who curry favor by appearing to be most like him. Yet Chénier
refused to pronounce in absolute terms. Just as monarchs have
drawn men of exceptional talent from the crowd, so too is the tyrant
compelled on occasion to heed the voice of the public when upright
men consent to become courtiers. It is undoubtedly this type of
thinking, the disinclination to speak of men in terms of a single all-
encompassing category, Chénier's description of a man as both
upright and a seeker of positions of favor, that led Scarfe to speak
of Chénier's "openness of mind" that "was forcing him into a
utopian position."[10] One might conjecture that the strength
of Chénier's belief in artistic freedom paradoxically led him to
recognize that given the right circumstances any form of government could be a potential haven for the arts. One has only to think

of the absolutism of Louis XIV where governmental regulation of the arts through the auspices of the French Academy was responsible for the flourishing of French Classicism. E. B. O. Borgerhoff has observed that the very undefinable nature of the *"je ne sais quoi"* to which seventeenth century French authors constantly alluded made French Classicism much more individualistic than is commonly assumed.[11]

Despite Chénier's favoring the republican form of democracy, he saw in aristocracy the most durable and tranquil of all the states and voiced his agreement with Montesquieu's conclusion that although moderation is its principle it has no need of virtue or good customs; "on the contrary it is in its interest and also its essence to destroy talents" (*Essai*, Pléiade, p. 631). And Chénier was quick to add that republics tend to forget that they were born of tyranny.

Both Montesquieu and Rousseau had written that the notion of a pure democracy was of little practical consequence. Chénier was in agreement but concluded, nonetheless, that "all talents are of the essence of democracy, a true republic" (*Essai*, Pléiade, p. 631). Although Chénier's attitude toward England in the late 1780's in the light of the social humiliations he endured there can hardly be classified as Anglomania, he did share his century's admiration for the English system of checks and balances described at length by Montesquieu.

Chénier then returned to the role of the artist in society. In a note, obviously incomplete because of his comment "develop that," Chénier spoke of the only circumstances which he thought inappropriate for the man of letters entering into public affairs: ". . . these are moments when the constitution is so corrupted, so full of former abuses . . . where the administration is so uniquely occupied with correcting only small details and where everyone is so frightened by the difficulties and troubles that a general reform would require and entail that cabinet members be feared" (*Essai*, Pléiade, p. 632). The situation described in this passage is not unlike that which Chénier confronted during the constitutional crisis of August, 1791, when his was one of the lone voices to be heard in favor of constitutional reform. If anything, Chénier's Revolutionary activity can be seen as a reversal of this statement, inasmuch as he judged it imperative to speak out with greater fervor at precisely the most chaotic moment.

In concluding this chapter, Chénier recalls the Voltaire of the *contes et romans* who suggested in various ways that the greatest dilemma confronting man was not great crimes — for, like Hobbes,

Voltaire believed that if all were bad man would have destroyed himself long ago — but rather the mediocrity of never having aspired to greater heights, that is, of accepting the status quo. Chénier wrote: "[the multitude] repents great crimes . . . because when, in a crowd of men, the moment of ardor is passed, reason and justice take over . . . but noted examples authorize faults, errors, stupidities which hardly revolt human nature and inner feeling is wiped out" (*Essai,* Pléiade, p. 632).

2. *"On Customs and Usages"*

Chapter III, "On Customs and Usages," which consists of only five fragments, is of interest chiefly because its remarks of a linguistic nature point to some of the ideas developed in "L'Invention." A fundamental aspect of Chénier's poetic theory was his belief in the need to accommodate universal human feelings in order to best express the particular truths of an age. The primary passions, he noted, are always the same. What changes in each century are customs, which accounts not only for the passions being manifested in different ways, but also for dramatic differences in languages. Chénier concluded from this that metaphorical language, the link between usage and things, constitutes a unique system in every nation and that this system, by virtue of its uniqueness, cannot be translated into any other language. Chénier's thoughts on language here contain in embryonic form the essence of his poetics, for in "L'Invention" he designated great art as that which is true to nature and expresses the primary, immutable human feelings in accordance with the changing content of each civilization.

C. *"Causes which are harmful to letters"*

1. *"On Literary Associations"*

The second part of the *Essai,* "Causes which are harmful to letters," is the most lengthy section. According to Chénier, there is virtually no haughtiness which approaches that of an author whom an academy has garbed with the magistrature of genius, a remark which suggests at once Voltairean satire and La Bruyère's use of portraiture, both of which techniques were used by Chénier.

The next subject is the previously quoted description of Chénier's childhood amusement in pretending to be a priest officiating at the mass.

One of Chénier's main arguments against literary academies is the

power they wield on aspiring writers. Not content to bask in his own
vainglory, the perpetual secretary of the Academy believes that he is
the "perpetual secretary" of the human race. Chénier's sparkling
satire, his ability to sketch an entire mode of behavior comprising
both social and moral qualities, stands as an example of eighteenth
century *caractères*. Bertrand's statement that Chénier's aesthetic
principle was radically opposed to that of the great classics is undoubtedly an overstatement inasmuch as Chénier shared the
seventeenth century's penchant for balance and decorum.[12] On the
other hand, his attack on literary academies was predicated on the
concept of artistic independence and with it the implied notion that
there remained fresh terrains for the modern poet to explore. Chénier's apparent debt to La Bruyère must be seen in its proper
perspective, for the author of *Les Caractères* had begun his most
celebrated work in complete opposition to Chénier's literary
philosophy by stating that "Tout est dit."

As Chénier indicated in his sketch on the "perpetual secretary,"
his examination of "literary associations" had been done in a spirit of
reform. Chénier's passing reference to the personal effects of
academicians and critics is significant inasmuch as it points to his
persistent fear that his work would be publicly attacked, an attitude
that accounts for his stating that the writer alone can be the judge of
his work. This fear of being publicly assailed explains also why Chénier chose to publish only two poems during his lifetime. His conception of literary independence and his espousal of self-judgment
as a viable critical tool was, of course, a far cry from anarchy. Unlike
Voltaire, however, whose battles with critics were legendary, Chénier did not have the temperament to engage in public disputes with
self-styled arbiters of taste and therefore elected to share his poetry
with a few intimates.

The central thesis of an extremely penetrating article written in
1914 by E. Chaponnière is that the eighteenth century salon, the
social extension of the academy, attempted to stifle expression of all
individual feelings and imposed a worldly philosophy, distinctly
epicurean in nature, whose ties to the present were by implication
incompatible with any sentiment of the past and which viewed the
art of literary criticism solely in terms of discovering faults.[13] It was
against this spirit that André Chénier directed his satire in Chapter
II of the *Essai,* and in so doing continued the tradition of Montesquieu in the *Lettres persanes* and Voltaire in the *Lettres philosophiques.*

2. *The indulgence of courts*

Artistic patronage fostered, in Chénier's views, a system of servitude in which the courtier must please his master, the king, just as the artist must please his master, the courtier. Hence, total instability prevails, inasmuch as favor is predicated entirely on appearance.

D. *"History of Style and Taste"*

The longest section of the *Essai*, the "History of Style and Taste," treats such subjects as the Bible, Voltaire, and modern writers. Chénier's lengthy discussion of the ancient Greeks contains the essence of his poetics and forms the basis for many of his ideas in "L'Invention."

1. *The Bible*

Biblical criticism was an eighteenth century preoccupation. The work of Bayle and Jean Meslier opened the way to a spirit of reform in which the authority of the Bible was subjected to an exhaustive scrutiny. No figure of the age is perhaps identified more closely with Biblical criticism than Voltaire. Voltaire objected to the Bible not only because of its breach against reason, but also because it had engendered fanaticism and superstition, perversions of the spirit of the earliest religions.

Chénier's criticism of the Bible took a different turn. Regarding the books of the Bible as the work of poets, Chénier saw in them a history of struggles and passions that were common to all poetry. Whereas Voltaire believed that the original moral intent of the Bible had been perverted, Chénier thought that its poetic content had been ignored. Like Voltaire, however, he felt that men of ignorance, greed, and monarchical ambitions had throughout history subverted the sense of the Bible according to their needs and that it was only through a historical accident that the books of the Bible were considered doctrinal works. Yet Chénier found that most people who rely on the Bible as a source of divine authority are unfamiliar with its contents. His views on the Bible were more in keeping with those of the English poet Milton than with those of the *philosophes* of his century.

2. On the Ancients

"The ancients were naked, their soul was naked. . . . For us it is quite the contrary. . . ." (*Essai*, Pléiade, p. 645). Martin Kopf has remarked that with the waning of the Quarrel of the Ancients and the Moderns toward the end of the eighteenth century there were no longer any deep-seated philosophical overtones linked with looking to the ancients for inspiration, and so writers returned to original sources in the hope that new life might be breathed into all forms of artistic expression.[14] Chénier's love of Greece had been nurtured by his mother and had resulted in his feeling a sense of destiny in the circumstances of his birth:

> A Greek woman, in the springtime of her youth,
> At the bed of a husband nourished at the bosom of France
> Caused me to be born French in the bosom of Byzantium.[15]

Indeed, antiquity was a common subject in eighteenth century literature. Montesquieu's *Considérations sur les causes de la grandeur des Romains et de leur décadence* had appeared in 1734 and Voltaire's historical writings were filled with pages on the ancients. Gourmont has stated that "Chénier loved Greece because for him it was the embodiment of the good and the beautiful."[16] Perhaps more than any other eighteenth century writer, Jean-Jacques Rousseau approached Chénier's love of antiquity as a period when the good and the beautiful meant simplicity, the enjoyment of rustic beauty. Estève's view that Chénier "liked nature in the manner of the ancients, as the refuge where one escaped from the noise and the inconvenience of the city"[17] seems equally applicable to Rousseau, as does Bertrand's description of eighteenth century attitudes towards antiquity: "some by a dillettante spirit, others by pure sincerity dreamed of frugality, simplicity, virtue . . . the dream of a real France reconstructed along the lines of the ancient city."[18]

Beyond Chénier's ethnic heritage and his sharing his century's interest in antiquity there lay his desire, as Kramer has observed, "to discern the methods whereby the ancients achieved perfection."[19] Whereas Rousseau's "Golden Age" was not temporally or spatially fixed, Chénier's ideal was definitely linked to a particular people in a particular age. His love of the ancients was motivated by his desire to apply their methods to his own artistic works, the basis for his theory of "imitative invention," which will be taken up at length in my discussion of "L'Invention." Chénier's Golden Age allowed him to escape the personal tribulations he encountered in eighteenth century France. His ultimate vision was directed toward his own times inasmuch as he felt that he must involve himself directly with his century as the ancients did with their century. He stated: "The Greeks were born for fine arts more than any other people in the world. They alone, in the frenzies of enthusiasm, always knew how to follow nature and truth" (*Essai*, Pléiade, p. 646).

Scarfe views this statement as an example of Chénier's prejudice in favor of the Greeks which "led him to scorn much of modern literature," but Kopf's assessment seems more accurate: "there is little or no attempt on Chénier's part to explain or validate his judgement of a given literary figure,"[20] the implication being that the role of intuition in Chénier's literary appreciation was considerable.

3. *The Realization of the Greek Ideal*

It is not surprising that the writers whom Chénier found distasteful were those who did not share the Greeks' penchant for simplicity and truth. They did not emulate nature. Among the writers Chénier placed in this group were Shakespeare, who was given to "barbaric convulsions" and "monstrous expressions," and the English poets, with the exception of Arthur Young, who had no model in nature. Several critics have noted, however, that Chénier's knowledge of English poets and English poetry was very limited. It is probably safe to conclude that he shared many of his countrymen's prejudices concerning English writers, including those of Voltaire who, in the *Lettres philosophiques*, described at length his reasons for disliking specific Shakespearean plays.

Artists of antiquity, according to Chénier, exercised not only their bodies but also their minds. In following the path of nature itself they penetrated the perfect beauty of nature. Chénier's description of the ancient sculptor illustrates his theory of creation amongst the Greeks. The Greek sculptor was above all a humanist. He was interested in everything that pertained to man and therefore read history and philosophy in addition to knowing human anatomy and psychology. He consequently was able to take nature's raw material — granite — and fashion it into a creation of his own making, into a work of art which captured an essence of man. Chénier's view of imagination here as something compatible with nature is in keeping with Saisselin's observation: ". . . it would seem that opinion concerning the imagination shifted, in the course of the seventeenth and eighteenth centuries, from associations with folly and madness to ones with creativity and nature."[21]

The qualities which Chénier listed as necessary for the production of great works of art reveal that he did not associate genius with unrestrained flights of fancy. Although being inspired by the works of antiquity is one indication of potential genius, in addition to being struck by beauty, having a penchant for solitary walks in the woods, and never being able to write as quickly as one thinks, there is also an indication that to be inspired means to work to one's fullest. The method incorporated into "L'Invention" is evident here; Chénier's discussion of the ancients was intended to serve a dogmatic function for the moderns and he therefore alternated between the two points of reference. Although Chénier understood Greek genius in terms of a patiently executed craft, his vocabulary in describing the Greeks — "burning imagination," "divine madness," "ardent chagrin" — shows that he approached them in terms of their sensitivity rather than their specific stylistic devices. Here and in "L'Invention" he wished to discover their method of perceiving the world, a method which if adopted by modern poets would render immortal the peculiar character of their own age: "Chénier found in the poetry of ancient Greece the most perfect expression of ideal beauty . . . what he asks of the Ancients, more than models and precepts, is the secret of life."[22] Dimoff notes the role of Chénier's masters at the Collège de Navarre in nurturing in their young pupil the love of Greece that his mother had first instilled in him.[23] Elisabeth Chénier had transmitted to André early in his childhood a pride in his Greek heritage which was further developed by the Hellenists in her salon and by his college studies.

Chénier's approach to Cicero was influenced in part by his appreciation of the Roman author's moral integrity. Curiously, Racine, whose odious character was legendary during his lifetime, was spared Chénier's moral indignation. Chénier preferred Corneille to Racine; he wrote that Racine had to live under Corneille's shadow but that Corneille had heights which Racine never achieved (*Essai*, Pléiade, p. 665). Maurras, however, sees the influence of both writers in Chénier's work and cites the Corneillean tone of certain counterrevolutionary ideas as well as the Racinian harmonies in Chénier's love poetry.[24]

Chénier's portrait of Cicero is balanced. Praising Cicero's benevolent character, his encouragement to other talents, and his concern for public welfare in a corrupt era, he concluded that there was a correspondence between the virtue Cicero extolled in his writings and the life he led. Chénier saw in Cicero the highest qualities which a man of letters could embody and which he hoped to implement in his own life — an enthusiasm for work, a sensitivity to beauty, a concern for public affairs.

Finally in this section, Chénier drew an analogy between the artistic life of a nation and that of an individual. Just as an artist's perversion of his own nature through outside influence leads to a lessening of his talents, so does the intrusion of foreign influence taint the intellectual milieu of an entire people. This, in his opinion, was what happened to Greece when she came under foreign influence.

4. The Moderns

In challenging the idea that the seventeenth century attained so great an excellence that it could not possibly be maintained and that what followed must automatically reflect a period of decadence, Chénier revealed that he championed exclusively neither the ancients nor the moderns. Genius was not limited, in his opinion, to a particular age, but could emerge at any time. Believing that the hallmark of his age was scientific and technological progress, he did not judge art from the concept of progress. Julian Eugene White, Jr. has noted that there was more latitude in the thinking of the two camps who comprised the Quarrel than has been commonly believed:

Actually, the more intelligent of the Moderns recognized the greatness of Homer, Virgil, and the other leading authors of Graeco-Roman antiquity. Boileau himself, leader of the party of the Ancients, could see more clearly than anyone else the greatness of modern writers such as Racine, Molière, Corneille and was certain that posterity would give them a place equal to the greatest ancients.[25]

White concludes that "in an even broader sense, the quarrel was a part of the debate between humanism and rationalism."[26] Chénier's desire to uncover the source of great art among the ancients, while celebrating the conquests of modern science and technology in his epic poems, represents an attempt to reconcile these two currents.

5. Voltaire

Voltaire was considered the greatest poet of his age. Poetry, during the Age of Enlightenment, was generally regarded as a precocious pastime and the consensus was that the poet revealed himself before reaching adulthood. Voltaire's evolution from poet to philosopher suggests that for the age philosophy represented a higher form of expression and that Voltaire's evolution was a natural process. Today, most of Voltaire's poems are seen to be pale Neoclassical imitations of the great works of the seventeenth century. Still, Voltaire was probably the most influential figure of his age. Although he undoubtedly had more enemies than any other contemporary writer, his admirers were legion and tended to deify his person. Thus, as Faguet points out, Chénier's generally negative feelings towards Voltaire were extraordinary around 1780.[27]

Chénier began his criticism of Voltaire by asserting that the very name of the deceased Voltaire will serve as a deterrent to would-be writers. Citing the continuing indiscriminate praise of "L'Henriade" as a type of literary enslavement, Chénier's reservations about Voltaire were not based primarily on literary considerations, but rather on what he considered to be Voltaire's lack of moral integrity. Although Chénier believed that Voltaire's enemies were a merciless pack, he attacked Voltaire for seeking the favors of the great, for his egoism and childish pride. At bottom, Chénier viewed Voltaire as a central figure in a continuing system of literary patronage. Mediocre people sought to enhance their own glory through contact with him, while Voltaire himself was a courtisan-author who flattered not only the king and princes but also their mistresses. Chénier's lifelong financial difficulties undoubtedly led him to attack Voltaire's boastfulness about his great wealth. Because he believed that Voltaire accumulated wealth at the expense of his independence, Chénier asked of Voltaire in a statement of questionable sincerity: "Does he want us to learn to prefer with all our heart the plumpness of opulent slavery to sober and independent poverty?" (Essai, Pléiade, p. 668).

Chénier felt that Voltaire's lack of honesty in dealing with his contemporaries was matched by a corresponding lack of profundity in his treatment of scientific and political questions and that his light sparkling style, amusing and stunning the reader, caused the reader to ignore his superficiality. What comes across in Chénier's assessment of Voltaire is that the critic was writing from the perspective of a moralist and was judging Voltaire in terms of his relation to, and influence on, the political, social, and economic institutions of his age. Typically, Voltaire as poet, as literary craftsman, is largely ignored.

6. *Influence of a bad literature*

Under the influence of religion man's critical spirit has been blunted. Religious books are taken to be infallible just as works of jurisprudence are considered sacred. Aristotle is criticized by Chénier because his works led to scholasticism. The most interesting aspect of this section is Chénier's remarks on Pascal. Like the Voltaire of the twenty-fifth letter of the *Lettres philosophiques*, Chénier attacked Pascal for using his talents "to uphold the most unrelenting sophisms" (*Essai*, Pléiade, p. 672). While admitting that there are eloquent passages in the *Pensées*, Chénier indicated that the contemplation of nature both in its grandeur and smallness was not for him, as it had been for Pascal, a source of anguish. Although Chénier's remarks on Pascal are brief, they are significant inasmuch as they reveal Chénier's fear of religious beliefs leading to the imposition of false and arbitrary conventions on humanity in the same way that academies foster literary conventions and tyrannical rulers impose political constraints. In all three domains nature and truth run the risk of being perverted. The attack on Pascal then must be seen in terms of Chénier's humanism. The famous Pascalian "wager" is detrimental because it is based on fear, the same fear which perpetuates unjust governments and literary patronage.

7. *Explanation of present circumstances*

The last chapter of the *Essai* deals most explicitly with Chénier's aesthetics. Before treating *"naïveté," "naïf," "imitation inventrice,"* and the nature of metaphorical language, concepts which form the heart of his poetics, Chénier developed once more his thoughts on affectation in literature. The French language, he stated, is artificial in the same way that the king of France is artificial. It aims at dazzling through preciosity and enigmatic expressions. Because French authors seek the sublime, natural expressions among their writings are very rare. Chénier then expressed his belief that most people do not have profound thoughts. Like Voltaire, he believed that most people do not avail themselves of their capacity to reason, but believe what the first charlatan tells them.

Believing that art and life must achieve an equilibrium, Chénier censured those who write generous and noble maxims, yet are delighted when writers whom they have praised are publicly disgraced. The originality of Chénier's aesthetics lies in his having insisted that the expression of nature in art is a reflection of the artist's integrity in the political and social spheres: ". . . it is necessary for the young man to count only on himself" (*Essai*, Pléiade, p. 679).

8. Naïveté

Chénier's guiding principle for all the arts — "homo sum" ("I am a man") — brings to mind the epithet chosen by the twentieth century humanist and moralist, Albert Camus, for *Le Mythe de Sisyphe:* "Oh my soul, do not yearn for eternal life but exhaust the domain of the possible." Early in the *Essai*, in his discussion of literary patronage and academies, Chénier had made it clear that he considered harmful to letters the fashionable and arbitrary pronouncements made by groups of men in the name of artistic infallibility. Now he attempted to define eternal values: ". . . nature and truth alone are eternal. . . . In the arts one must be true with force and precision, that is to say, one must be naïve. . . . *Naïveté* is the point of perfection of all the arts and of each genre in all the arts" (*Essai*, Pléiade, p. 675). Although Chénier never set down in exact terms what he meant by a naïve thought, his commentary on the authors whose works he cited as examples of naïve thought, including Corneille, Racine, La Fontaine, Montaigne, Montesquieu, Rousseau, Virgil, and Horace, reveals that he regarded *naïveté* as the quality of possessing and communicating "an infallible erudition of nature, a profound and naïve experience of the human heart" (*Essai*, Pléiade, p. 683). He adds that "there are sentiments so pure, so simple, thoughts so eternal, so human, so much ours, so profoundly innate in the soul, that the souls of all readers recognize them instantly" (*Essai*, Pléiade, p. 684) *Naïveté* for Chénier was linked with the primary primordial feelings of love, hate, and fear. The naïve artist is a consummate connoisseur of human nature through his study of the moral and intellectual world and of his own heart. The concept of *naïveté* does not attempt to deal with the question of progress in art. Chénier recognized what escaped many at the time, the fact that the theory of progress cannot be applied to creative works of art.

The implications of *naïveté* are far-reaching. It is an expression of Chénier's belief that civilization is built on continuity and universally shared experiences, on the one hand, and elements that reflect the age and the artist's unique personality, on the other. What has been frequently overlooked in the debate about the degree to which Chénier was a partisan of the ancients or moderns or of imitation or invention is the fact that the modern writer who aspires to greatness is compelled to be creative inasmuch as the truly naïve writer cannot be imitated. The great writers of the past can and should serve as sources of inspiration by virtue of their being wellsprings of human feelings which they are able to communicate through understatement. It is significant to note, moreover, that Chénier envisaged nature's eternal truths in affective terms. He was surprisingly modern in his positing psychological theories of projection and identification. On the other hand, such abstract matters as versification, prosody, and rhythm are to be found neither here nor in other works dealing with poetics.

In another passage illustrative of his psychological modernity Chénier cited the changes wrought on the human personality as a basis on which a doctrine of tolerance and understanding might be built. Like the Rousseau of the *Confessions* (Book III) who wrote "if each man could read in the hearts of all other men there would be more who would want to be humbled than rise,"[28] Chénier was aware of the complex submerged layers that contribute to human behavior at any point in a person's life: ". . . I hold that this history would not be less important to study than another, nor less efficacious in teaching us the art of doubting, of tolerating . . ." (*Essai*, Pléiade, p. 685). Whereas Rousseau's alluding to life's stories which each of us must bear silently in our hearts was an attempt at self-vindication and an effort to elicit sympathy from the reader, Chénier saw in the complexity of human behavior a source of potential unity among men. As Saisselin has remarked: "Rousseau the citizen of Geneva was perhaps the only true anti-artist who ever lived . . . on moral grounds he coherently and thoroughly opposed the entire world of art he knew, which everyone else accepted almost without question."[29] It would be grossly inaccurate to say that Chénier accepted the entire world of art without question but, on the other hand, his criticism reflected an ameliorative spirit that was directed at a greater integration of life and art. In this respect he did not merely follow his age but stood in the forefront.

9. *Chénier's theory of metaphysical language*

Earlier in the *Essai* Chénier had pointed to the weaknesses of the French language: "The French language fears poetry" (*Essai*, Pléiade, p. 672). He went on to blame French authors for having borrowed unwisely from antiquity with the result that their works lacked natural expression. But the weaknesses of the French language were not innate: ". . . it admits everything but it refuses the presents of those whom it hardly knows and who mistreat it" (*Essai*, p. 688). The French language has infinite possibilities for those who have worked to familiarize themselves with its nuances. It is only when he has mastered his language that an author can impose his inimitable stamp on universally experienced emotions. New combinations can always be formed from nature's fecund storehouse.

The same expressions, born independently in different minds, are never exactly duplicated when an author has searched for new ways to synthesize nature's eternal truths. Chénier's theory of creation was based on the concept of the metaphor. Like the Greek sculptor of antiquity who worked with nature's sources in order to create a unique work that was distinctly his, the modern author must find new ways to communicate universally felt emotions and concepts. As stated in this *Essai* and elaborated in "L'Invention," Chénier's concept of *naïveté* is linked to "inventive imitation." Great art by definition springs from nature and nature is eternal. (". . . this network of good works . . . far from exhausting the source, sustains it and reproduces it, since the forms of human minds are as varied and inexhaustible as those of faces" [*Essai*, Pléiade, p. 690].) Immortal works of art are at once linked together by their common origins and nature and by the expression of their creators' unique juxtaposition of nature's elements. They therefore have physiognomies no less distinctive than the faces of the artists who composed them.

Chénier's belief that artists invariably reveal their psychological makeup in their works is perhaps the most specious aspect of his argument, but he had undoubtedly anticipated objections to this theory when he dismissed as inferior those artists whose works were not in harmony with their life. Thus, Chénier's poetics centered about a theory of creativity in which art and nature and man and art are in perfect balance.

In his *Essai* Chénier sought a middle ground between Bayle who, in elevating Cartesian rationalism to new heights, paved the way for eighteenth century liberalism and freedom from the past, and writers such as Le Brun, Jean-Baptiste Rousseau, and even Voltaire, whose epic poems were highly imitative of Corneille and Racine. Rejecting the notion that the theory of progress can be applied to creative works, Chénier regarded nature in terms of universal human experiences and the artist's individuality. As defined in the

Essai, the poet's mission was to glean nature's eternal truths amidst the shifting political and social background of his age. Chénier conceived of civilization, therefore, as the expression of permanent moral values which the artist must embody in his works.

In the *Essai sur les moeurs* Voltaire had decried man's lack of moral progress throughout history and had in fact concluded that mankind had become more barbarous throughout the ages. Chénier was not primarily concerned with a chronological account of man's moral record but rather with establishing a sense of continuity in what he considered the basic traits of human nature which belong to no one and to everyone. This, he believed, was the artist's imperative and he therefore opposed elements that would define the future by effacing the past. Chénier's role as a preserver of civilization is already evident here, the ideology that will explain most of his activity during the Revolution.

II   *"L'Invention"*

The most complete and most popular of Chénier's doctrinaire works, "L'Invention," is a poetic manifesto which, manuscripts indicate, was written in 1787. Although Chénier undoubtedly worked on the *Essai* long after completing this poem, the *Essai* was begun first. In many respects "L'Invention" is an elaboration of ideas contained in the *Essai.* Chénier divided his poem into five principal sections: (1) a condemnation of imitation; (2) a definition of original invention; (3) a program of what the poet's function must be henceforth; (4) a refutation of the objections that one can make to this program; (5) a conclusion.

As Clifton Cherpack has pointed out, "L'Invention" is no less a poem because of its doctrinal quality and must be read with an eye for its organic unity and formal autonomy. Viewing "L'Invention" from this perspective, Cherpack sees Chénier embracing "antithetic and apparently unreconciled points of view."[30] Cherpack's view is shared by other critics, such as Margaret Gilman, who wrote that Chénier's doctrine indicates an antagonism between content and form.[31] From the discussion of this poem it will be seen that "L'Invention" is the focal point of Chénier's writings and has elicited the most controversy.

A.   *The condemnation of servile imitation*

At the outset of his poem Chénier stated that the true poet is an inventor: ". . . Life is promised only to inventors." The images in which he couched his theory are those of ancient continental Greece, referred to as Attica. Here there existed a spirit of peace and harmony that was favorable to the production of great art: ". . . un ciel pur, les plaisirs, la beauté, Des Moeurs simples, des lois, la paix, la liberté, Un langage sonore. . . ." (". . . a pure sky, pleasures, beauty, simple customs, laws, peace, liberty, a sonorous language" ["L'Invention," Dimoff, 5 - 7]). When Chénier spoke of *moeurs*, he seems to have thought above all of social conventions which remove man from nature, the sole entity capable of inspiring the poet. As he had written in the *Essai:* "The ancients were naked, their soul was naked, for us it's the contrary" (Pléiade, p. 645). The Greeks themselves were inventors and therefore erected the first column of the temple of art.

Modern poets must erect their own columns. Yet modern poets run a risk in imitating the *method* of the ancients because, in Chénier's mind, antiquity is nature itself. Nature's bounty is endless but in this very quality lies the impetus for the poet to try his own hand in extracting her riches: "Essayons d'épuiser la source inépuisable" ("Let us try to exhaust the inexhaustible source" ["L'Invention," Dimoff, p. 60]). Chénier's plea for the erection of new columns is inspired by the splendor of the ancients' first column erected on the temple of art. His attitude towards antiquity is in fact the embodiment of the Neoclassical ideal. Chénier's affinity with certain aspects of the Neoclassical aesthetic is seen in his response to the first of five possible objections, the idea that invention means the joining together of disparate elements. Chénier refuted *"l'esclave imitateur"* ("the slave-imitator"), he who, as characterized by Du Bellay, merely imitated half-lines of Virgil.

But immortal arts cannot be imitated. Those who attempt to do so produce inferior works. What must be imitated is the spirit of the ancients, their understanding of human nature, their respect for genres, their adherence to good sense. Those who would view invention as a right to group disparate elements are guilty of a "mad delirium." Thus, after having celebrated the inventive spirit of antiquity, Chénier counsels the modern poet to erect new pillars for the temple of art, which is as inexhaustible as nature from which it draws its materials. Chénier's philosophy of art, as in the *Essai*, was predicated on eternal values which lend continuity to the changing political, social, religious, and artistic conditions in which works of art are produced.

Because nature is inexhaustible, the ancients could not possibly, in

Chénier's eyes, have held the only key to producing immortal works of art. The poet, audacious enough to write an epic according to new formulas, is compared to the navigator who plunges into the waters in the hope of discovering new lands. The analogy between the inventor and the navigator which is sustained throughout the poem suggests that for Chénier the true inventor is a discoverer, one who sees in nature what had always existed but which his discerning eye alone can communicate. Although Chénier's reverence for the past was motivated by his conviction that the moderns too create immortal works, he suggested that only in assimilating the spirit of the ancients can the process of original imitation be achieved. For the artist who has the gift of creation the ancients can teach the secret of seizing nature.[32]

B. *Toward a definition of original invention*

The inventor is the man gifted with a powerful imagination who has nature produce what she would have been able to create in her combinations but which in fact she didn't create. Thus, Chénier counselled the rendering of natural models more expressive and more logical:

> . . . dans les arts l'inventeur est celui . . .
> Qui, fouillant des objets les plus sombres retraites;
> Etale et fait briller leurs richesses secrètes;
> Qui, par des noeuds certains, imprévus et nouveaux,
> Unissant des objets qui paraissaient rivaux,
> Montre et fait adopter à la nature mère
> Ce qu'elle n'a point fait, mais ce qu'elle a pu faire. . . .

> . . . in the arts the inventor is he
> Who, extracting from objects the most somber haunts
> Displays their hidden riches and makes them shine;
> Who, by certain associations, unforeseen and new,
> Uniting objects which appear in conflict,
> Reveals to nature herself and has her adopt
> What she has not done yet but what she might have done. . . .
> ("L'Invention," Dimoff, pp. 60 - 61)

Chénier's theory of the disparate rapports which exist in nature recalls in its modernity Baudelaire's *correspondances* ("Nature is a vast temple where living columns sometimes allow confused words to escape." ["Correspondances," Pléiade, p. 87]) and Proust's description in *A l'ombre des jeunes filles en fleur* of how the different young girls who were members of Albertine's group constituted a model of beauty which transcended the traits of the individual members. The influence of Condillac, whom Chénier studied in college, and who wrote in the *Essai sur l'origine des connaissances humaines* that "we don't really create ideas, we only combine them," is evident here.

Chénier went on to say that near the chariots of the ancients the modern poet must make his own imprint. That Chénier was one of the first to impose a sense of history on the classical doctrine is seen by his statement that the ancients have finished the complete course of their development, whereas the moderns are only at the beginning of their civilization. He then described the conquest of the earth by human science by signalling some of the progress attained by physics and natural history in uncovering the "secrets of the earth" just as astronomy has uncovered the "secrets of the sky." The celebration of modern science is linked to Chénier's concept of poetry here, the invention of a universe by the invention of a language. For those who continued to write traditional poetry, science (truth) was one thing and poetry (fiction) was another. The moderns must act, by availing themselves of natural resources, as the ancients would act were they alive today.

Chénier gave a place of merit to great writers of the seventeenth and eighteenth centuries. He showed that the merit of the ancients was to depict their soul and that of their contemporaries and that subsequently the glory of the moderns must consist in painting the modern soul. What he objected to in his century's Neoclassicism was its imitation of seventeenth century models. The ancients, he maintained, should be studied not to be imitated but rather so that their art might be learned, so that the moderns might borrow not their ideas but their colors.

In none of this discussion did Chénier introduce a theory of progress in the arts. Genius, he felt, was not limited to time or to space. The idea of perusing the beauty, style, and color of the ancients, their good taste and fidelity to nature suggests that imitation must apply only to form. Indeed, Chénier maintained that the ancients should remain the masters of the moderns' form but not of their thought. This *"innutrition,"* a term derived by Emile Faguet, suggests so thorough an assimilation of the ancients' modes that the modern is no longer able to distinguish them from his own substance.[33] He should never forget that his world is different from that

of the ancients, yet he should depict his world as an ancient would
were he suddenly transported into the eighteenth century. It isn't
enough therefore to know how to think, one must also know how to
feel.

Chénier's doctrine revolved around an aesthetic of taste. His concept of history would have led him to support what Saisselin has
called a *"goût de comparaison"* (a penchant for comparison),
". . . the discernment of characteristics which differentiate civilizations and works of art in time and space."[34]

C. *The poet's function*

The poet, the new navigator who, unlike the navigator of old, has
modern instruments to guide him, must use his skill to transmit an
intense collective emotion. Chénier evoked the fury of the *pan-
égyries*, the manifestations of the collective soul of the entire Greek
people. In this way would he render for posterity the soul of a
civilization. He alone, in seeking new associations in inexhaustible
nature, can change the flowers of antiquity into honey for the
moderns. This idea of gathering what previously existed in the manner of bees who hover from flower to flower to create substance that
is uniquely theirs — honey — is summarized by the most celebrated
line Chénier ever wrote: "Sur des pensers nouveaux faisons des vers
antiques" ("Let us graft ancient verses onto new thoughts"
["L'Invention," Dimoff, p. 65]). This line and what immediately follows are illustrative of Chénier's doctrine of "inventive imitation."
For Chénier, the mythological explanation of the universe was lacking in reality and logic. The modern poet must reject the ancients'
fables, gods, and futile lies inasmuch as nature, which is in us "the
source and the model" is now seen in terms of mechanical and
physical laws. Nature alone, taken as a source and model, allows the
creation of *chefs d'oeuvre*. Chénier counselled the young poet to
choose unknown subjects in order to reap the more dazzling glory of
putting them at the feet of his contemporaries. Modern science
provides the poet with sublime images:

> Quel amas de tableaux, de sublimes images,
> Naît de ces grands objets réservés à nos âges!

> What an accumulation of tableaux of sublime images
> Arising from these great objects reserved for our ages!
>
> ("L'Invention," Dimoff, p. 64)

The ancients, if alive today, would themselves grasp the fecund riches which modern technology provides. The system of nature appears in its imposing majesty and we are far from the conceptions of Epicurus and Lucretius. Although Chénier believed in scientific progress as the basis of new poetic inspiration, he did not view this new subject for poetry as an automatic sign that the modern poet would be more inspired than the ancient and would thus produce more brilliant verse. The mission of the poet, Chénier believed, was to express the hallmarks of his civilization. Modern science would provide the necessary degree of enthusiasm for the poet to reveal himself in the plenitude of his humanity. By "grafting verses of antiquity onto new thoughts," the modern poet would imbibe the spirit, the inspiration, the enthusiasm that the ancients had felt in contemplating their universe and rendering it immortal by transforming their vision into a work of art. It is thus that André Chénier wished to be "a Greek poet in French."

D.   Refutation of objections to his doctrine

Chénier structured his poem in the form of a dialogue between an interlocutor and an unknown auditor who apparently interrupted periodically to voice his objections to the doctrine. The first objection, one that embodies that portion of the classical doctrine embraced by Boileau, was that invention, conceived as the right to pile up disparate elements without principle or restraint, was an offense to truth, good sense, and reason. Chénier had countered this fear by stating that he conceived of the inventor as one who, far from yielding to "wild outbursts," was able to bring together divisive elements in harmony and therefore depict what anyone might have been able to feel in the same manner. The idea that the true inventor knows how to uncover beauty hitherto undiscovered in seemingly insignificant objects was already cited in the Essai.

The second objection is that nature has established genres which were respected by the Greeks and which proscribe any blending of tones. Chénier responded by asserting that a creative reconciliation of things does not involve a violation of fixed genres. He then focussed his attention on the dangers of writing epic poetry which he compares to those of Thésée entering the labyrinth. The verb "côtoyer," which means "to keep close to shore," used here and elsewhere, enabled Chénier to distinguish between those who hover excessively about the banks claimed by the ancients and those who are determined to head for the open seas. The sails for coastal sailing are different from those needed for the open sea, just as the spirit of the true inventor who accommodates diverse images through creative metaphorical language is different from that of the poet who is content to tread familiar ground. In countering the objection that the ancient civilizations were more favorable than the modern for the production of great art, Chénier developed a different attack from that used in the *Essai*. In the earlier work he had written: "Many people believe falsely that in attacking not mythology itself but the abuse of mythology . . . one wants to therefore proscribe antique allegories" (*Essai*, Pléiade, p. 692).

What Chénier meant by abuses consisted of treating the gods of Olympia as real figures capable of controlling at their will the workings of the universe. His reference to the progress made in the world of science when compared to the "puerile world of ancient mythology" does not imply that he viewed the progress of art linked to the progress of science. The ancients were able to create immortal works because they expressed their concept of nature as they knew it. The moderns, on the other hand, must express nature as they know it, nature whose workings, explained by a simple game of forces and mechanical and physical laws, are "austères, moins grands, moins pompeux" ("austere, less glorious, less pompous") than the "belles chimères" ("beautiful illusions") of antiquity. Scientific progress challenges the poet to create works of art that reflect the changes in his civilization. If the ancients, inspired by a nature badly known, were able to produce great works, what will the moderns do? Chénier did not dismiss these complaints, but rather encouraged the poet to embark on a long and arduous journey. If he accepts the challenge of poetically transmitting abstract scientific theories his triumph will be all the more dazzling.

The vision of a world viewed in terms of scientific laws gives rise to the fear that the new discoveries of science are not accessible to a public who cannot understand difficult technical language. This objection allowed Chénier to describe in detail his conception of the process of poetry. Poetry can translate even the most abstract ideas by dressing them in colors and in dazzling images. Admitting that certain modern scientific theories, enveloped in clouds, are less easy to expose with clarity, he insisted, nonetheless, that an author incapable of independent thought finds only a void ("L'Invention," Dimoff, p. 67). The art of the poet can fix fleeting thoughts and states of the soul:

Elle sait même encore, ô charmantes merveilles!
Sous ses doigts délicats réparer et cueillir
Celles qu'une autre main n'avait su que flétrir . . .

It knows how to repare and even gather,
Oh charming marvels, under its delicate fingers,
Those which another hand has known only how to stain . . .
("L'Invention," Dimoff, p. 67)

Chénier then gave a detailed description of the origin and formation of amber as an analogy of the poet's power to entrap potentially
fleeting elements and fix them for posterity in his verse. An insect is
encased in sticky resin and then washed into the sea and turned in
time into amber by the actions of salt water. The image of water as a
metaphor of man's passage in time was seen in Chénier's comparing
the modern poet to a navigator who must chart new courses, and was
continued in the theory of the formation of amber. It was sustained
for a third time when Chénier, evoking the image of water flowing
through hidden rocks which change its substance, suggested that the
poet should seize nature's turbulent elements and thus create a universe through his unique metaphorical language.

In his final injunction to the modern poet Chénier stressed three
times the necessity of work. This emphasis on work was undoubtedly
prompted by Chénier's own habit of working on several projects at
one time and leaving them unfinished. His own reference to his
"vagabond muses" can be seen as a regret on his part that he was not
often given to the discipline required to bring a poem to fruition.
Chénier believed that only in work could poetry add the last hand to
the conquest of the universe by science in glorifying it. The great
poet, like the sculptor of genius, thus brings to life ignored treasures.
Through his enthusiasm and hard work the poet has the potential
with his "docte ciseau" ("learned chisel") to follow and find life and
the soul and all its traits. The poet is the marble thinker in whom the
divinity lives.

In dealing with the fifth conceivable objection to his theory, the
belief that the French language is unequal to the challenge of
creating a modern epic, Chénier abandoned the previously used
structural device of having his interlocutor respond to a critic of his
theory. Chénier now asked the question himself, "Oh language of
the French! Is it true that your destiny is to grovel always and that
you alone are wrong?" ("L'Invention," Dimoff, p. 70.) In "L'Invention," as in the *Essai*, Chénier affirmed unequivocally that defects in

works written in French are not inherent in the French language and must therefore be blamed on the authors. Citing a long list of authors who have in his mind written works of lasting value despite the alleged inferiority of their working language — Le Brun, Racine, Despréaux, Rousseau, Buffon, and Montesquieu — Chénier insisted once again that it was incumbent on the poet to innovate. How can a pale language be remedied if the poet is afraid to enrich his vocabulary? The French language, he went on to say, is weak in its shadings and vocabulary only to modern authors who blame their language when the thoughts which they wish to express are unclear. Such writers are not worthy of the name poet; they are mere rhymers. The inspiring genius of the poet is personified by Chénier in the form of a divinity. His language, enflamed and controlled by a true demon, "imprévu, dans son âme produit" ("unforeseen, produced in his soul", ["L'Invention", Dimoff, p. 71]) no longer is his own private domain:

> Les images, les mots que le génie inspire,
> Où l'univers entier vit, se meut et respire,
> Source vaste et sublime et qu'on ne peut tarir,
> En foule en son cerveau se hâtent de courir. . . .
> Tout s'allie et se forme, et tout va naître ensemble.

> Images, words, which genius inspires,
> Where the entire universe lives, stirs, and breathes,
> A vast and sublime source that cannot be exhausted,
> Hasten to run in a crowd in his head. . . .
> Everything is united and formed and everything is
>   going to be engendered together.
>
> ("L'Invention," Dimoff, p. 71)

To invent, therefore, in Chénier's mind is to conceive a great design, the plan of an edifice not yet constructed.

E. *Conclusion*

In concluding, Chénier warned that the new poetry will not come easily. Citing Cicero who wrote that language is a soft wax in the hands of those who know how to use it (which recalls the inventor as a sculptor who creates anew from previously existing matter, just as the bee creates honey from nectar), Chénier argued that the French language consents to fold only under adroit hands. The different languages and dialects which have evolved are in Chénier's view the result of such complex factors as variations in the evolution of speech organs according to climate. More important, however, the state of French poetry is not dependent on the French language. A people is not the servant of its language: language owes its character in large part to the people who use it. Having stated that the modern poet must express himself in his work in order to prove that he is aware of the most recent scientific theory, Chénier evoked a vision of civilization as a process perpetually in a state of becoming. The status quo is impossible to maintain if French poets must rise to the challenge of expressing the new cosmos in their work or "ramper dans la fange" ("grovel in the mud").

In "L'Invention" Chénier wished to create an epic from science. Convinced that science as well as mythology could inspire the poet, he sought to renew for modern civilization the tradition of vast primitive poems in which the vision of the universe was transformed into an artistic vision through the poet's imagination. Chénier's view of civilization as a process involving both continuity and evolution has led some critics to speak of the tone of uncertainty in "L'Invention" when Chénier spoke of the doctrines of imitation and invention. As stated in the poem, however, Chénier saw the true inventor as one who peruses the ancients in order to set the course for his own explorations into unknown territories. As a statement of the literary values Chénier uncovered in the *Essai*, "L'Invention," a poem of vast erudition and convoluted turns, proclaims that neither taste nor inspiration can be said to belong to any one specific age.

III   "Epître sur ses ouvrages"

The "Epître sur ses ouvrages" was begun in 1787, a period when Chénier was working on many of his major works, including the *Essai*, "L'Invention," "La République des Lettres," "L'Hermès," and "L'Amérique." Whether the *épître* was addressed to Le Brun or not remains a matter of critical debate. The prose draft of this work, addressed to de Pange, points to the discussion of Chénier's work habits that were developed in the poem. Chénier had originally intended to write an *épître* to de Pange on the occasion of the latter's departure for Switzerland, but inasmuch as the piece wasn't completed in time and would not have had the intended sense after de Pange's return, Chénier decided to rework the poem, deleted the long section referring to de Pange's travels, and concentrated instead on describing his method of work.[35]

The prose draft, beginning with Chénier's lament at the departure of his friend, contains a statement which reveals not only Chénier's views on the subject of friendship, about which he was unabashedly sentimental, but the great difficulty he encountered in maintaining the discipline required to complete a work. Comparing himself to a hobbyhorse who moves incessantly or to a potter who, intending to make a jug, creates a teacup, Chénier remarked that his thoughts are centered on "L'Hermès" for one instant, then on "L'Amérique," and finally on a foolish elegy. His capricious imagination takes him everywhere, but ultimately leads him back to his original projects. Thus Chénier's method of composition can be compared to the creation of a vast mosaic. Sketches and designs are outlined and are filled in after a long passage of time during which new travels, loves, and friendships have intervened. This approach to writing suggests the method which in "L'Invention" was characterized as that of the true poet, one who is forever reaching out beyond obscuring clouds in order to grasp and elucidate diverse elements in nature.

Chénier's originality lay precisely in this method of composition which consisted of going from individual details to the completed work rather than the contrary. In the verse form of his *épître* he revealed two sides of himself, the one comic, the other serious. The work, moreover, stands as a model of satire inasmuch as Chénier used to perfection the ploy of attacking, while professing not to yield to the temptation of pointing to, the injustice and hypocrisy of his times. He began by stating that satire has always been appreciated by the French because it fulfills the psychological need of thinking oneself superior to others. Satire, he added, aims at bruising while one laughs and he, for one, takes no pleasure in smashing a fool. The works of foolish authors carry with them a self-indictment; further ridicule is unnecessary and critics who attack in a spirit of vindictiveness reveal only their own feelings of inferiority.

Chénier then went on to distinguish himself from such satirists-critics. His pleasures are elsewhere, although he finds countless material for satirical writing in France. Those who deserve to be the subject of attack are instead praised by fawning poets who, wishing to be rewarded, flatter them. At the same time that Chénier here denounced satire as an unworthy form of composition he imitated Boileau's caustic wit, but used the social and political satire of

Juvenal and Archilocus rather than the literary satire of Horace or Boileau. Although Chénier did not develop at length his invective against specific social abuses, the fact that he unequivocally asserted here his distaste for literary, as opposed to political, satire foreshadows the mentality that was to take root in the *iambes*.

In describing his method of work, Chénier rendered in verse form many of the ideas of the prose draft. He described himself as working on the thousands of objects his eyes have noted, pushing them and storing them for future reference. Then, at the proper time, these objects, having incubated long enough in his head, burst forth in independence like newly hatched chicks who flit and run to the woods. Like the sculptor, Chénier works not in broad strokes but in measured movements as he chips away at the massive material before him. Chénier attempted to justify his method by comparing it to the foundryman's. His works can take form only after arduous preparation, just as the clockmaker who prepares the molten bronze has only to run the liquid into the proper molds for clocks of different sizes to be formed:

> Moi, je suis ce fondeur: de mes écrits en foule
> Je prépare longtemps et la forme et le moule,
> Puis sur tous à la fois je fais couler l'airain:
> Rien n'est fait aujourd'hui, tout sera fait demain.

> I am this foundryman: from my writings in a throng
> I prepare at length both the form and the mold,
> Then I make the bronze flow on everything at once:
> Nothing is done today, everything will be done tomorrow.
> ("Epître," Dimoff, vol. 3, p. 205)

These lines are highly revealing of Chénier's conception of art. Poetry was for him neither a social game aimed at pleasing nor a vocation which isolated man from his environment. Like the foundryman's bells that told of both death and approaching daylight, poetry, a microcosm of civilization, requires arduous preparation before it can be delivered to its public. Chénier's disinclination to publish his works in the belief that he needed more time to perfect them suggests that he was motivated by pride and that he himself was his most exacting critic. If he sought glory through his works he wished to merit it rather than conform to standards of taste that would damn tomorrow what had been praised today.

The last section of the poem summarizes the elements common to metaphors of the metal worker and sculptor. Civilization, of which art is a primary component, does not involve destroying the riches of the past but weaving them into the fabric of one's own work so that, like an invisible seam, they are not evident to the naked eye. This creative imitation or innutrition allowed Chénier to form his own substance from among the materials he had combined.

Chénier ended his poem by satirizing poets who will undoubtedly attack him for having pilfered from Montaigne the metaphor of bees creating their own substance from the nectar they gather. Although the tone of sections of the "Épître sur ses ouvrages" distinguishes it from "L'Invention," both works proclaim that the similarity of thought and expression among authors separated by centuries, the basis of naïve thought, is not inconsistent with originality. Here, as elsewhere, Chénier advanced a philosophy of art in terms of his view that civilization comprised stratified layers of man's most glorified achievements.

IV "La République des Lettres"

Toward the end of 1786 and the beginning of 1787 Chénier had been contemplating writing two short satires, one on the baseness and servility of poets of his time, the other on the jealousy and bad behavior of poets. The idea of combining these two satires into a single one probably came about because of the unfavorable critical reception given his brother Marie-Joseph's play *Azémire*. In protesting against the ignorance and incompetence of certain critics, Chénier suggested that he foresaw a day when he might be similarly treated. "La Republique des Lettres," titled by Dimoff, is one of Chénier's most personal works. It shows that in his search in the *Essai* for essential relationships between literature and society and in "L'Invention" for a means of reconciling the spirit of the ancients with the new cosmos of the moderns, Chénier never ceased to uphold a humanistic orientation, one that was man-centered.

"La République des Lettres" is concerned with the man behind the poet. It constitutes a testament of faith to the extent that it reveals Chénier's most cherished personal principles. The poem begins with an affirmation of Chénier's love of independence. The movement of the poem is one of contraction based on an opposition between the worldly environment which corrupts the poet's integrity and the well-being experienced in the confines of his private

Louvre where, in his sparsely furnished room, he plants the harvest
that he wishes to gather. Poetic material must be gathered and
stored. It must not be subject to the whims of a few. Here he can
peruse the world in his books and assimilate the rich substance of
human experience. His enterprising hive is filled with the rich nectar
of his multifarious interests: "Tout m'enrichit, et tout m'appelle, et,
chaque ciel/ M'offrant quelque dépouille utile et précieuse
("Everything enriches me and everything calls me and each sky
offering me some useful and precious bounty. . . ." ["La République," Dimoff, vol. 2, p. 208]). His attitude toward material
possessions evokes both Villon and Rabelais:

> Une pauvreté mâle est mon unique bien.
> Je ne suis rien, n'ai rien, n'attends rien, ne veux rien.

> A manly poverty is my sole good
> I am nothing, have nothing, await nothing, want nothing.
> ("La République," Dimoff, vol. 2, p. 208)

What follows appears to be a denial on Chénier's part of any interest
in politics:

> Quel prince est libéral, et quel est méchant homme,
> Est un soin qui jamais ne troublera mon somme.

> Which prince is liberal and which one is evil
> Is a concern which never robs me of sleep.
> ("La République," Dimoff, vol. 2, p. 208)

Yet this apparent disinterest in political affairs is immediately
qualified when he expresses his disdain for writers who are only
poets and who are ignorant of everything that is not poetry.
Although Chénier envisaged his Louvre as a place where he might
retreat from the machinations of worldly society, he did not proclaim
an "art for art's sake" manifesto that would later be adopted by the
Parnassians. In "L'Invention" he similarly hinted at the relationship
between art and the political and social environment in which it is
produced ("all the arts are united"). Chénier's idea here, to be taken
up in the twentieth century by Albert Camus in "Jonah," is not that
the artist must detach himself from society and social concerns but
that the rigorous discipline involved in the creative act demands assimilation of the artist's thoughts, experiences, and readings and that
the act of creation requires at least a temporary retreat. Like Camus,

Chénier first believed that the artist could remain detached from political influences but soon became aware that art could evolve freely only if certain basic safeguards of man's collective existence were preserved. Having dismissed as "foolish toys of a worrisome drive" those whose interests and knowledge are confined to poetry, Chénier then railed against the tenor of his century's negative critical spirit. "Nul n'est juge des arts que l'artiste lui-même" ("No one is a judge of the arts but the artist himself" ["La République," Dimoff, vol. 2, p. 211]).

Art was therefore for Chénier not a game reducible to a formula. At the court where men profess to love all the arts and attempt to reveal themselves patrons of the arts by contemplating in silence three hours each day, genius is allied with the ability to curry political favor. Such a climate is totally unfavorable for the birth of individual enthusiasm from which great art must emanate. Chénier's ideal of the *honnête homme* was one who recognized and avoided the dangers of hypocrisy and false reasoning. For Chénier genius carried with it a high degree of responsibility.

Chénier believed that the poet has a mission to perform in society — he must act as a seer and guide humanity to a better life. To accomplish this end the artist must immerse himself in as wide a range of the disciplines of art and science as possible. Chénier's conception of art therefore transcended the partisanship that surrounded much of the debate associated with the Quarrel of the Ancients and the Moderns. Both camps, in his opinion, had produced self-proclaimed guardians of artistic standards who were motivated only by their own vainglory. Whatever talent they possess is marked by their defects of character. For Chénier the artist should not be separated from the man. Diderot alone in the century, in such works as *Le Neveu de Rameau*, shared Chénier's interest in the relationship between the artist and his work.

The eleventh section of the poem consists of a Molièresque portrait of the so-called young poet for whom art is more a social grace than a gift of the soul. Treated with as much curiosity as Montesquieu's Persian, the poet banters and the crowd laughs with delight, composes impromptu verse with dessert which is called a marvel, and finds that his words are admired even before he speaks. With this type of modern imbecile Chénier contrasted the artists of antiquity, such as Tibullus and Gallus, who maintained their independence and therefore their integrity by knowing how to work far from the crowd.

Whereas in "L'Invention" Chénier was more concerned with the relationship between the form and the content of poetry and the environment in which it emerges, in "La République des Lettres" he attacked many of the prevailing practices of authors in order to focus on the qualities he most admired in an artist. The essence of Chénier's artistic credo, stated here, has above all moral implications: "Respecte la vertu, les lois, le diadème;/ Mais sache aussi toujours te respecter toi-même." ("Respect virtue, laws, the diadem; But always know how to respect yourself" ["La République," Dimoff, vol. 2, p. 231]).

Chénier's words were directed against fashionable salon poets who were more eager for social success than for writing great verse. The genius of antiquity was not a matter of language but a disposition of being, free men acting in a free society. As a humanist the poet must have knowledge of the major movements and ideas of the past that have molded his civilization, but he must not be deterred from the exacting task of bringing his creative vision to fruition. This he can do only in the privacy of his own thoughts. The poet, in Chénier's view, must now isolate himself from society. Although he is a potential critic of society his first critical impulse must be self-oriented, for he is the ultimate judge of his works. "La République des Lettres" therefore qualified the major premise of the *Essai* and "L'Invention." The Greeks may have been born for the fine arts; they flourished in an environment in which artistic independence was cherished. To the contemporary poet, however, Chénier offered the dictum to create his own haven in the midst of social and political forces which would destroy his individuality. Liberal art from antiquity meant those studies worthy of a free man. This is the concept which Chénier upheld as an ideal.

In "La République des Lettres" Chénier expounded his views on the artist and society. In attempting to define the political, social, and economic forces which influence a writer, Chénier distinguished between the kind of patronage and influence which he felt were detrimental to the production of great art and the artist's interest in maintaining the institutions of a free society that would enable him to uphold his integrity. "La République des Lettres" then is a blueprint for Chénier's writings during the Revolution in its affirmation of the mutual interdependence of the artist and society.

V *Le Commentaire sur Malherbe*

In 1842 Chénier's annotated copy of Malherbe was discovered by Tenant de Latour who had it published that same year by the

Bibliothèque Charpentier in an edition of Malherbe's works. Chénier's commentaries, which constitute a document of literary history
of the greatest interest, can be divided into several categories: (1)
those which consist of diverse comparisons and citations borrowed
from other poets, both ancient and modern; (2) those which relate to
questions of taste; (3) a few commentaries dealing with a study of
Malherbe's language; (4) a single note dealing with Malherbe's
metrics.

As a document the *Commentaire sur Malherbe* reveals the
enthusiasm of the eighteen year old Chénier and, as Kopf has noted,
represents, even more than his other critical and theoretical works, a
sincere and spontaneous *profession de foi*, for if Chénier believed in
the primacy of inspiration he was a disciple of Boileau with respect
to the necessity of perusing the great works of the past in order to assimilate their images, enthusiasm, and balance, in short, the elements which constitute their genius.[36]

It is Malherbe's lyricism that Chénier first praised. Significantly
lyricism was not defined by Chénier in terms of the poet's intimate
thoughts but rather as an indication of Malherbe's familiarity with
the French language which in turn enabled him to create sonorous
and harmonious sounds. If Chénier praised the musicality of
Malherbe's language, he criticized a line of "Les Larmes de Saint-
Pierre" ("The Tears of Saint Peter") for combining two unrelated
metaphors, suggesting therefore that unlike many nineteenth century poets he considered integration of form and content a standard
of great poetry as opposed to mere beauty of sound. The image that
is developed in "L'Invention" and other works, that of the poet as a
sculptor who creates his own work from pre-existing sources or the
bee who makes honey from the nectar of various flowers, is
foreshadowed in Chénier's stating that one of Malherbe's charming
images, which has become common, is expressed in a fresh manner.
What is at issue here is Chénier's belief that a great artist distinguishes himself not so much by the content of his work, for the
passions are universal, but rather by his finding new ways to express
eternal ideas. The concept of art as a continually building process, in
which new layers are added to earlier layers, suggests the importance of art in man's history and foreshadows Chénier's thesis in
"L'Hermès" where the development of the arts and sciences is
linked to man's civilizing impulses and striving towards greater
happiness.

Chénier's interest in the musical quality of Malherbe's verse extended to Malherbe's rhythmic innovations as well as to his

philosophical reflections. The commentary on specific expressions used by Malherbe testifies to the scope of Chénier's erudition and to his penchant for details.

In other ways the *Commentaire sur Malherbe* points to Chénier's poetic output of the 1780's. His later statement that "l'astre qui fait aimer est l'astre du poète" ("the star which makes one love is the poet's star" [Dimoff, vol. 3, p. 138]) was already influencing his work inasmuch as his remarks on Malherbe's "Fin d'une ode pour un roi" make a claim for the primacy of inspiration: "He had foreseen that he could terminate several odes by a few strophes of this genre, which enthusiasm and delirium make excusable and even pleasing in great poets" (*Commentaire*, Pléiade, p. 820).

The *Commentaire sur Malherbe,* no more systematic in structure than the other works dealing with poetics, is nonetheless a valuable document. It reveals that Chénier viewed poetry as an exacting discipline in which the personal stamp of enthusiasm would be integrated with observance of rules which had been associated with works of the immediate past. In its definition of poetry as a reflection of all aspects of human activity, embracing necessarily the intellect and the emotions, it indicates more fully than any other work how inappropriate are such labels as "last of the classics" and "first of the romantics," which the nineteenth century applied to Chénier.

CHAPTER 3

The Bucolics

THE term bucolic was originally used as a synonym of pastoral. Virgil's ten pastoral poems, to which the term "eclogue" is now generally applied, were called "bucolics" by the grammarians. During the Renaissance and seventeenth century there was a tendency to reserve the term bucolic for Virgil's eclogues and for the imitations of these specific works of Virgil. Since pastorals of the Virgilian tradition portrayed people of culture and refinement, the critics insisted that it would be more accurate to use the term bucolic when referring to poems of this type.[1]

No group of Chénier's poems has been the subject of more controversy than the bucolics. The problem is not merely that of the date of composition, for it must be remembered that Chénier dated very few of his works and questions of chronology therefore arise with respect to most of his poems. His intended grouping of these poems presents a more serious problem.

In my discussion of ten representative bucolics, in which I have used Dimoff's categories, I have stressed unifying thematic and structural elements in view of my belief that these poems constitute a single grandiose project in which the poet availed himself of the decor normally associated with bucolics merely as a point of departure, thereby depicting not only young lovers in pastoral settings but the violence of uncontrolled nature and passion.

The earliest specimens of André Chénier's poetry, dated October and December, 1778, are bucolics, "Xanthus," in imitation of Homer, and "Médée," in imitation of the eighth eclogue of Virgil. From 1779 until the Revolution interest in antiquity in France was greatly intensified through the impetus of archeological excavations which had an influence on sculpture and painting and in translations of Winckelmann's *History of Ancient Art*. In addition to imbibing the color of Greek customs in his mother's salon, which was fre-

quented by such Hellenists as the poet Le Brun, the academician
Suard, and Brunck, editor of the *Anthologie Grecque*, André Chénier came into contact with the writings of the major Greek and
Roman authors of antiquity while a student at the Collège de
Navarre. Throughout the century, moreover, the virtues of pagan
culture had been upheld by such writers as Montesquieu and Rousseau with no less fervor than that shown towards the English system
of government. It is not at all surprising then that Chénier's literary
beginnings should bear the mark of antiquity. Each bucolic evokes a
tableau or series of tableaux, striking by their forceful simplicity. As
one reads the bucolics, it is apparent that the seas or fields against
which the scenes unfold do not give rise to idyllic joys; premature
death, mothers weeping over the bodies of their sons, murder committed by jealous lovers — these are the recurring subjects of Chénier's poems. Love, friendship, solitude, death constitute the affective sources of the bucolics.

I   *Chénier's First Bucolic:*
"Xanthus" (Heroes and Fables)

Chénier's first poem concerns the death of a young handsome
warrior, Xanthus. Written when Chénier was sixteen, this poem
demonstrates a concern for detail and technique that characterizes
all the bucolics. The use of proper names four times in this poem of
eleven lines creates an intense, closed atmosphere, rendered
awesome and mysterious by the use of the definite article with the
name Xanthe, the dead Xanthus' mother. The first three words of
the poem, "le beau Xanthus" ("the handsome Xanthus"), is Chénier's use of a single condensed epithet to suggest more than one
quality. Xanthus is not only handsome but young and vigorous and
the contrast between this physical portrait and the fourth word of
the poem, "succombe" ("succumbs"), renders his death unexpected
and, consequently, all the more moving. Chénier's skillful modifica-
tion of the alexandrine by use of *enjambement* conveys the steady,
uninterrupted movement of Xanthus' soul "en flots de sang sur la
terre épandue" ("spread out on the ground in waves of blood"
[Dimoff, vol. 1, p. 47]). The poet's habit of practicing inversion, considered one of the ways to distinguish poetry in the eighteenth century, is evident here and serves to heighten the drama of Xanthus'
death; literally "Du mont Ida jadis au Xanthe descendue" ("From

Mount Ida formerly from Xanthe descended" [Dimoff, vol. 1, p. 47]). In a space of three lines the nobility of motherhood is evoked:

> Le Xanthe le vit naître, et lui donna son nom.
> Il expire loin d'elle, et sa reconnaissance
> Ne paiera pas les soins que coûta son enfance. . . .

> The Xanthe saw him born, and gave him his name.
> He expires far from her, and his gratitude
> Will not pay for the cares that his childhood cost.
> (Dimoff, vol. 1, p. 47)

In this section Chénier did not describe Xanthe's grief but allows us to imagine it, thus heightening the dramatic impact of her son's death by alluding to filial affection that will never again be forthcoming. The rhythm, moreover, of the ninth, tenth, and eleventh lines, with two *enjambements* and uneven groupings of syllables with many pauses, suggests the slow, yet inexorable progression of death:

> Faible, à peine allumé, le flambeau de ses jours
> S'éteint: dompté d'Ajax, le guerrier sans secours
> Tombe. . . .

> Weak, scarcely lighted, the torch of his days
> Is extinguished: tamed by Ajax, the warrior without help
> Falls. . . .
> (Dimoff, vol. 1, p. 47)

In the conclusion the abstract and the concrete are once again juxtaposed ("un sommeil de fer accable sa paupière" — "a sleep of iron overwhelms his eyelid" [Dimoff, vol. 1, p. 47]), while Chénier's use of an adjective with sensual overtones ("palpitant") underscores Xanthus' last efforts to affirm life before his final stage of evanescence: "Et son corps palpitant roule sur la poussière" ("And his palpitating body rolls on the dust" [Dimoff, vol. 1, p. 47]).

Explaining the particular charm of the bucolics Lanson concluded: "The themes, ideas, images of his favorite poets have been employed artistically by him to express his own nature, his own emotions. . . . The experience of Chénier is based on his erudition; and in his verse modeled on the ancients ("vers antiques") what he writes is not always "new thoughts" ("des pensers nouveaux") but, at the very least, personal feelings of observed nature."[2]

II "Nymphe tendre et vermeille, ô jeune Poésie"
(Poetic Invocations)

Addressing himself to Poetry in this work Chénier revealed, through use of apostrophe and metaphor, his conception of art. After having lauded Poetry from the perspective of the Ancients, Chénier, continuing his apostrophe, turned to the present. The effect is that of having introduced another personage. As is frequent in the bucolics, harmony results here from the musical opposition between two voices.[3] The same young Poetry is addressed here but the sensual quality of the first tableau, as evinced by the series of visual images relating to color, clothing, precious metals, and music, has given way to a series of questions. The rhythm of these lines is no longer languishing and heavy but heavily accented and rapid, heightened by Chénier's continued use of inversion:

> Nymphe tendre et vermeille, ô jeune Poésie,
> Quel bois est aujourd'hui ta retraite choisie?
> Quelles fleurs, près d'une onde où s'égarent tes pas,
> Se courbent mollement sous tes pieds délicats?
> Où te faut-il chercher? Vois la saison nouvelle.

> Tender and ruby red Nymph, o young Poetry,
> What wood is today your chosen retreat?
> What flowers, near a wave where your steps wander off,
> Are bent softly under your delicate feet?
> Where must one seek you? See the new season.
>
> (Dimoff, vol. 1, p. 3)

Chénier's evocation of springtime is conventional. The white face of winter has been replaced by the sparkling purple color of the new season:

> L'hirondelle a chanté. Zéphire est de retour.
> Il revient en dansant. Il ramène l'amour. . . .

> The nightingale has sung. The warm spring wind has returned.
> It returns dancing. It brings with it love.
>
> · (Dimoff, vol. 1, p. 3)

What attracts our attention is not Chénier's imagery but his having imbued both Poetry and the seasons with animation, a technique developed further in his presentation of the earth as the daughter of Jupiter. Poetry is invested here with primordial qualities. In a series of images reminiscent of the lines he wrote in the early 1780's describing his childhood visit to a fountain near Limoux which he described as the source, Chénier depicted the earth as eager to give forth melodious verse just as the winding river unfolds soft, sonorous liquid. In an extremely complex image Chénier asserted that verses nurtured by the rays of the sun *are* (as opposed to "give rise to") "ce peuple de fleurs au calice vermeil" ("this people of flowers with a red chalice" [Dimoff, vol. 1, p. 4]). What has happened here is that Chénier, in a level of abstraction not unlike that of Maurice Scève, conceived of an inanimate image, the earth, as instrumental in giving rise to another inanimate image (verse), which is immediately identified as people of flowers. These last elements are not elucidated but further shrouded in mystery, that of the blood and body of Christ during Communion (the chalice). Springtime, verse, and communion are all linked by a common futurity, a harvest not yet gathered, a generation of readers not yet born, and the hope in an afterlife which can never be validated. Poetry, a function in this work of primal forces — water and sun — is nonetheless always beyond man's grasp, suggesting more than it states with certainty, and it is in this duality, of which this poem is itself a splendid example, that the magic and vitality of poetry lie.

III *"L'Aveugle"* (Singers of Chants)

The composition and conception of "L'Aveugle" ("The Blind Man"), notes Félix Gaiffe, rested on a belief in the personal existence of Homer and shows that Chénier did not take into account the widespread eighteenth century controversy on the subject of Homeric poetry.[4] The increasing number of translations of Homer and other ancient authors after 1770 by no means meant that the reading public was able to penetrate the spirit of the ancients, for, as Gaiffe points out, the exploits of Homer's characters, as depicted by Chénier's contemporaries, were frequently a travesty.

The poem is structured into three main sections, an introduction (lines 1 - 148), a second part constituting the poet's recitation (lines 149 - 256), and a conclusion.

A. *Part One*

Chénier conferred a sense of authenticity to his poem by com-
mencing directly with Homer's words instead of providing narrative
description. Homer's three entreaties to Apollo in these lines create
many rhythmic pauses and communicate the urgency of his quest:

> Dieu, dont l'arc est d'argent, Dieu de Claros, écoute,
> O Sminthée-Apollon, je périrai sans doute,
> Si tu ne sers de guide à cet aveugle errant.
>
> God, whose arc is silver, God of Claros, listen,
> O Sminthus-Apollo, I shall undoubtedly perish,
> If you do not guide this wandering blind man.
>
> (Dimoff, vol. 1, p. 66)

Chénier's adjectives, moreover, assume affective values. The epithet
"faible" ("weak") of the fifth line is opposed to the "abois tur-
bulents" ("turbulent barkings") of the shepherds' hounds, yet the
musicality of the mute e's at the end of lines five and six ("pierre-
terre" — "stone-earth") as well as the circumlocution used to
describe the shepherds ("enfants de cette terre" — "children of this
earth") counter the initially hostile environment suggested by the
dogs' barking. The linking of abstract adjectives with abstract nouns
in lines nine and ten ("fureur indiscrète," "faiblesse inquiète" —
"indiscreet furor," "troubling weakness") underscores the mystery
and uncertainty of Homer's arrival amidst the shepherds', an
impression which is heightened by the series of questions asked
by the shepherds about their unknown visitor. Dramatic intensity is
sustained here through Chénier's subtle use of antithesis: the poet's
physical traits ("Quel est ce vieillard blanc, aveugle et sans appui?"
— "Who is this white-haired old man, blind and without support?"
[Dimoff, vol. 1, p. 66]) and his "ceinture agreste" ("rustic outer gar-
ment" [Dimoff, vol. 1, p. 66]) are contrasted with "les sons de sa
voix" ("the sounds of his voice") which "émeuvent l'air et l'onde et
le ciel et les bois" ("move the air and the wave and the sky and the
woods" [Dimoff, vol. 1, p. 66]).

The rapid succession of verbs used to evoke the poet's actions ("il
entend leurs pas, prête l'oreille, espère,/Se trouble, et tend déjà les
mains à la prière" — "he hears their steps, listens, hopes, falters and
lifts his hands in prayer" [Dimoff, vol. 1, p. 66]) heightens the uncertainty of the confrontation between youth and old age. The affective

and hyperbolic language by which the three shepherds address the poet ("vieillard infortuné," "mortels malheureux," "ta voix noble et touchante" — "unfortunate old man," "unhappy mortals," "your noble and moving voice") is in opposition to the turbulence of their mastiffs' uncontrolled barking and comforts the blind old man.

Addressing himself directly to the shepherds the poet, having heard the young men speak, defines them in terms of their youth ("Enfants, car votre voix est enfantine et tendre" — "children, for your voice is childlike and tender" [Dimoff, vol. 1, p. 66]) while referring to himself in the third person (". . . l'indigent étranger/ Croit qu'on rit de ses maux et qu'on veut l'outrager" — ". . . the poor stranger/Believes that people scoff at his afflictions and that they wish to insult him" [Dimoff, vol. 1, p. 67]). The august, noble language beginning at line twenty-nine is rapidly transformed into the poet's simple declaration: "Je ne suis qu'un mortel, un des plus malheureux!" ("I am only a mortal, one of the most wretched!" [Dimoff, vol. 1, p. 67]). He goes on to state that he has not aspired to frequent the realms of the gods as did Thamyris, who was blinded after boasting that he had overcome the muse, or been punished, like Oedipus, for having committed parricide, but has known the purely terrestrial misery of darkness, exile, poverty, and hunger. The food given the old man becomes a symbol of the bounty reaped by the virtuous ("le pain de pur froment, les olives huileuses, le fromage et l'amande, et les figues mielleuses" — "wheaten bread, olives laden with oil, cheese, almonds, and honey-drenched figs" [Dimoff, vol. 1, p. 67]).

Despite his contention that he is no more than an unfortunate mortal who has endured life's vicissitudes, Chénier's Homer speaks here in the prophetic, moral tones of a god of antiquity, praising the shepherds for their goodness and foretelling their reward: "Vous croîtrez . . . grands, féconds, révérés,/Puisque les malheureux sont par vous honorés" ("You will grow . . . great, fecund, honored,/ Since unfortunate men are honored by you" [Dimoff, vol. 1, p. 68]). The shepherds whom Homer meets, unlike the shepherds of "La Liberté," are free, free as children of the earth, to tender the fruit of this earth to those in need, free to perceive the harmony and wisdom of Homer's voice. Chénier's use of epithets here deserves attention inasmuch as he creates a universe of unequivocal moral dimensions, primarily by his orchestration of simple words through repetition and inversion;

. . . . Vous êtes beaux tous trois.
Vos visages sont doux, car douce est votre voix.
Qu'aimable est la vertu que la grâce environne!

. . . . You are all three handsome.
Your faces are gentle, because your voice is gentle.
How pleasing is the virtue that grace surrounds!
                                                    (Dimoff, vol. 1, p. 67)

The poet's inner narrative, which begins at verse seventy-six, permitted Chénier to achieve the harmonious contrapuntal effect of two
distinct voices here, that of Homer and that of the shepherds. Of
note in this section is Chénier's sense of the dramatic implicit in his
not mentioning Homer by name until the last line of the poem and
in his creating a striking relationship between form and content in
the language he uses to reveal the blind man's recollection of certain
sounds. In addition, Chénier's penchant for arranging adjectives in
groups of threes is seen in the description of the "riches grossiers,
avares, insolents" ("vulgar, greedy and insolent rich men" [Dimoff,
vol. 1, p. 68]) who do not possess the mental disposition to discern
talent just as the bloodthirsty vultures to whom they are likened are
unaffected by the pure and light voice of the nightingale. Interior
rhymes and alliterations create a distinctly musical quality to this
passage: (". . . Grossiers, . . . insolents . . . sentir . . . glissante . . .
seul . . . silence . . . mugissante . . . puis j'ai pris cette lyre, et les
cordes mobiles ont encor résonné . . . lorsque d'énormes chiens, à la
voix formidable . . ." [Dimoff, vol. 1, pp. 68 - 69, italics added].
Homer terminates this section of his account by imploring the gods
in whose goodness his belief has never wavered. The beauty and
wisdom of Homer's voice in Chénier's tableau are thus inseparable
from his moral attributes. Dramatic intensity is in fact sustained
throughout by the contrast between the barbarity of the blind man's
tormentors and the moral purity of their victim, a juxtaposition
which allows Chénier the opportunity to glorify poetry.

Chénier's concept of the poet as a moral legislator and his belief in
the mutual dependence of the artist and society — the poet must
sing the glorious accomplishments of his age for the benefit of
posterity — were elaborated in such works as the *Essai*. Although
Chénier's Homer was not immortal from the point of escaping
human vicissitudes, he did walk with the gods by virtue of the purity
of his song and the profundity of his moral insight.

The feast to which the youths invite the old man evokes a tableau

of traditional mythological splendor ("un siège aux clous d'argent
. . . le miel et les bons vins,/Sous la colonne où pend une lyre
d'ivoire" — "a chair with silver nails, honey, good wines,/Under
the column where an ivory lyre hangs" [Dimoff, vol. 1, p. 69]). At
this point in the narrative, Homer becomes a symbol of the eternal
quality of great poetry, for although his body is exhausted by sorrows
his voice remains vibrant, and he thus evokes scenes that encompass
every facet of man's existence — poetry, the gods, war, rustic
pleasures, and the dead — concluding with a glorification of the
poet's inspiration. Chénier's Homer then is a venerable old man who
is at once an idealist and a conciliator, seer and bard in one, who
modulates his song to accord with the deepest needs and desires of
men in their troubled history.

B. *Part Two*

Homer's description of human scenes, including a series of images
embracing the arts, government, war, in short all aspects of
mankind's activity, is not reported directly but is stated as descriptive narrative, a variation that allowed Chénier to focus attention
more specifically on the old man's auditors and the effect of his
divinely inspired poetry on them, underscored by the use of the present tense: ("il poursuit").

> Il poursuit; et déjà les antiques ombrages
> Mollement en cadence inclinaient leurs feuillages . . .

> He follows; and already the ancient shadows
> Were softly bending their leaves in cadence . . .
> (Dimoff, vol. 1, p. 70)

Chénier depicted men and nature both spellbound by the unknown
poet in their midst. The seemingly inexhaustible source of the poet's
knowledge is evoked through Chénier's using the conjunction "et"
("and") thirteen times within a space of twenty-four lines. The
plastic quality of this art is very much in evidence. The series of
scenes describing the Trojan War suggest that Chénier viewed the
world as a visionary through the eyes of a painter and sculptor before
thinking and feeling:

> Et le sang plus qu'humain venant rougir la terre,
> Et les rois assemblés, et sous les pieds guerriers . . .

Et les mères en deuil, et les filles captives . . .
Les chansons, les festins, les vendanges bruyantes . . .

And the more than human blood coming to redden the earth,
And the assembled kings, and warriors under their feet . . .
And mothers in mourning, and daughters captive . . .
The songs, the feasts, the noisy harvests . . .

(Dimoff, vol. 1, p. 71)

Beginning at line 183 Chénier's Homer is no longer conceived as a personage modelled on reality, but rather as the ancient creator of the "Iliad" and "Odyssey," whose power to see and order the elements of nature causes his auditors to believe that he is the prime mover of these elements. The same songs of death conclude, however, with a lyrical incantation in striking contrast to the fury of uncontrolled nature, hitherto evoked by the old man:

Mais, ô bois, ô ruisseaux, ô monts, ô durs cailloux,
Quels doux frémissements vous agitèrent tous
Quand bientôt à Lemnos, sur l'enclume divine,
Il forgeait cette trame irrésistible et fine . . .

But, oh woods, oh streams, oh mountains, oh hard stones,
What gentle shimmerings move you all
When soon at Lemnos on the divine anvil
He forged this irresistible and fine thread . . .

(Dimoff, vol. 1, p. 72)

The last section of Homer's account described the battle of the Lapiths and Centaurs, a vivid and intense narrative punctuated by the use of *enjambement*. Chénier's presentation of the fury of war through the use of accelerated rhythms represented a shift from the plastic, picturesque art of earlier lines and is essentially an art of movement. It recalls Racine's use of rhythmic changes and vowel patterns to paint the horror of Hippolyte's death as recounted by Théramène in *Phèdre*. Heredia's having borrowed the same lines from Ovid as the basis of two sonnets which are even more concentrated than Chénier's lines suggests that the ancients, Chénier, and the Parnassians represent three distinct stages in the evolution of poetic art.

C. *Conclusion*

The four references to the transcendental quality of the blind man's verse in the fourteen lines that constitute the conclusion — "saintes mélodies . . . paroles divines . . . prophète éloquent . . . disciple aimé par les Dieux" — "holy melodies . . . divine words . . . eloquent prophet . . . disciple loved by the Gods" (Dimoff, vol. 1, p. 74) — reflect Chénier's attitude toward Homer and the epic poetry of antiquity. Inspired by Ovid as well as by Homer, Chénier's primary interest was not in recreating the factual elements of Homer's blindness or relating specific details found in the "Iliad" or "Odyssey." In "L'Aveugle" Chénier elevated the art of poetic narrative to the level of suggesting rather than describing feelings and emotions. He achieved this effect by his creation of swiftly changing tableaux which function as verbal bas-reliefs. Homer's offerings, a "tissu des saintes mélodies" ("fabric of holy melodies" [Dimoff, vol. 1, p. 74]), constituted a microcosm of human existence, Chénier's own "Seven Ages of Man," in which rustic feasts and joyous young maidens, blood-stained warriors and inspiring lyres, all form part of the tapestry.

IV *"La Mort d'Hercule"* (Heroes and Fables)

The subject of the death of a young hero allowed Chénier to achieve the lyrical grandeur of "Xanthus." The story of Hercules' death is as follows: Dejanira made her husband Hercules wear a tunic which she believed would make him faithful to her, but which in reality was drenched with the poisoned blood of the centaur Nessus. Tortured by agonizing pain, Hercules burned himself alive on the top of Mount Aetna and took his place in Olympia.

Chénier's apostrophe of Mount Aetna through the first half of the poem conferred a cosmic aura on the scene of Hercules' self-immolation:

Oeta, mont ennobli par cette nuit ardente . . .
. . . Ta cime épaisse et sombre
En un bûcher immense amoncelle sans nombre
Les sapins résineux que son bras a ployés.

> Etna, mountain ennobled by this ardent night . . .
> . . . Your thick and somber summit
> In an immense funeral pyre piles up innumerable
> Resinous pines that his hand has bent.
>
> (Dimoff, vol. 1, p. 43)

The use of verbs in the present tense to describe Hercules' actions — "il y porte la flamme. Il monte." — "he carries the torch there. He climbs." — conveys the slow willful movement by which Hercules will be consumed amidst the towering trees he had once bent. Hercules becomes the embodiment of strength and consummates in his death the state of being a God by his resolve in the face of destiny. Chénier's use of understatement and the successive *enjambements* at the conclusion underscore the inexorable annihilation of Hercules' body by the flames. It is in fact the very simplicity of Chénier's style that adds a lyrical, poignant quality to this canvas of death:

> Le vent souffle et mugit. Le bûcher tout en feu
> Brille autour du héros; et la flamme rapide
> Porte aux palais divins l'âme du grand Alcide.

> The wind blows and roars. The funeral pyre all ablaze
> Shines around the hero; and the rapid flame
> Carries the soul of the great Alcide to the divine palaces.
>
> (Dimoff, vol. 1, p. 43)

If the death of warrior-gods in Chénier is not fearsome it is not stoical either. Hercules' apotheosis, at once noble and poignant, suggests Sisyphus' resignation to his fate while anticipating the grandeur evoked by Alfred de Vigny in "La Mort du Loup" and "Moïse."

V   *"Pannychis" (Love and Lovers)*

"Pannychis" is one of Chénier's most striking portraits of childhood purity. This poem, having little in common with the sensuousness of the work of antiquity bearing the same title, reveals eighteenth century influences as well as the more tender side of Chénier's nature. Eighteenth century artists such as Greuze had sentimentalized children in their paintings of bourgeois family life, but "Pannychis" evokes more specifically the ethereal side of Watteau's and Fragonard's paintings as well as the stylized depictions of childhood in the work of Jean-Jacques Rousseau.

The charm of this poem lies in its expression of innocence. In the prose preface to the poem, the love a five year old boy feels for his cousin Pannychis has no reality beyond the rose bushes that surround the boy. The scene of the boy's revelations of his feelings, a copse, inspires his imagination, and the words he uses to describe his love evoke both discretion and expressiveness:

> Oui, je l'aime, Pannychis . . . Elle est belle . . . Nous nous
> promenons sous cet ombrage . . .
> Je lui ai donné une statue de Vénus que mon père m'a
> faite avec du buis. Elle l'appelle sa fille, elle
> la couche sur des feuilles de rose dans une écorce
> de grenade.

> Yes, I love her, Pannychis . . . She is beautiful . . .
> We walk under this shade . . . I have given her a
> statue of Venus that my father made for me of wood.
> She calls it her daughter, she sleeps it under rose
> petals in a pomegranate bark.
>
> (Dimoff, vol. 1, p. 91)

Childhood innocence in the verse section is closely identified with nature. This is the only world that is known to the little boy and, as he begins his song to Pannychis, he attempts to persuade her of his worth by speaking of living things in his environment. He has grown taller than his goat and is prepared to give Pannychis a nutshell as a safe dwelling. Theirs will be a life filled with the riches of nature: a large shell packed with earth will yield flowers whereas holly-oak bark thrown on their pond will serve as the boy's fleet.

The image of a docile war horse with which the poem ends adds a note of ambiguity in its suggestion that the boy's longing for a lasting idyllic existence is chimerical, for even in the world of mythology toy horses give way to gigantic steeds carrying warriors to battle.

VI *"J'étais un faible enfant"*
(*Children, Young Boys and Girls*)

"J'étais un faible enfant" ("I was a weak child"), a song in praise of youthful love, relates the feelings of a young boy for an older girl.

Whereas "Pannychis" was situated in the present, the young boy of
this poem is already a mature man. The accumulation of verse in the
imperfect tense reveals that the world of pure feeling and beauty has
vanished (". . . mon innocente main/ Parcourait ses cheveux, son
visage, son sein" — ". . . my innocent hand/ Ran over her hair, her
face, her breast" [Dimoff, vol. 1, p. 102]), the paradise of childhood
is lost. Childhood, however, is a moment that one wishes to pass.
Just as Pannychis' lover tried to impress her with his size, implying
greater maturity, this singer of love regarded himself unfavorably
with respect to his beloved: "J'étais un faible enfant qu'elle était
grande et belle" ("I was a weak child when she was big and
beautiful" [Dimoff, vol. 1, p. 102]). Even to the eyes of a child, obstacles are an important factor in keeping love alive, for the girl
never seemed more appealing than when she was seen before her
other admirers. The joys of this age are never fully appreciated
because they are fleeting.

Certain aspects of Preromantic sensibility are evident here.
Whereas Chénier celebrated with nostalgia the joys of youthful love
he did not engage in the glorification of suffering through love that
was to become a dominant theme in the works of the generation of
1820. His love scenes recall in miniature the *fêtes galantes* of his century. Undoubtedly, Chénier's evocation of young love in a pastoral
setting had a marked influence on Victor Hugo who, in removing all
vestiges of ancient shepherds in his poem "Lise," nonetheless
evoked the same expansiveness, the same naturalness that resulted
from the love of a young boy for an older girl, another love quick to
bloom and quick to fade.

VII   "La Jeune Locrienne"
(Children, Young Boys and Girls)

"La Jeune Locrienne" begins with a four-line translation of a
Locrian song celebrating free love in which a young girl who has
committed adultery bids her lover to make a hasty departure before
he is discovered. Chénier's use of "nous" ("we") throughout his narrative foreshadows Flaubert's use of the same pronoun in the opening sentence of *Madame Bovary*, which created similar effects of
direct observance of the action as well as uncertainty by the fact that
the identity of "we" is never revealed. The modulation of voices on
different registers is accomplished here by the contrast between the
narrator's acceptance of the young woman's mores ("Nous aimions
sa naïve et riante folie" — "We liked her naïve and fun-loving

madness" [Dimoff, vol. 1, p. 105]) and the words of her accuser: "Locriens perdus, n'avez-vous pas de honte?" ("Fallen Locriens, have you no shame?" [Dimoff, vol. 1. p. 105]). The zealous Pythagorean's appeal to "maximes austères" ("austere maxims") and the rewards reaped by virgins (Chénier's use of the word "vierge" — "virgin" — does not always have a figurative meaning) represent the voice of self-restraint in worldly matters and imply that men have the constancy to adhere to such discipline. Chénier's own brand of sensualism, posited on a belief in human fickleness, is suggested by the sudden tear that forms on the black eye of the chastized woman (a color evoking adversity and constraint) that just as quickly gives rise to gaiety and songs as she leaves with a new lover, a young Thurien, as handsome as she is beautiful. The poem shows a Chénier who was at once a disciple of the ancients' doctrine proclaiming the need to integrate mind and body, the spiritual with the material, as well as a supporter of his own century's resuscitation of the doctrine of natural man. Although hardly a libertine, Chénier shared certain aspects of eighteenth century worldly sensualism and did not hesitate in his personal life, as well as in some of the elegies, where literary convention appears, to oppose absolute and rigid standards of behavior with the ways of the world.

VIII *"La Jeune Tarentine"* (*Marine Idyls*)

"La Jeune Tarentine," the first poem to be published after Chénier's death, was at that time given the title "Elégie dans le goût ancien" ("Elegie in the ancient manner") by the poet's brother Marie-Joseph. The popularity of this work is seen in its having been reprinted numerous times between 1801 and 1808. The most anthologized of Chénier's works along with "La Jeune Captive," "La Jeune Tarentine" has been categorized as a marine idyll by Dimoff and others, but it is at the same time an epigram in the classic sense of the term. That is, it is meant to constitute the text of an inscription found on a tombstone.

The reading public of the Napoleonic era was well prepared to react favorably to this poem. The two principle sources of this piece were of an esoteric nature, Manilius in *Astronomiques*, where the author speaks of the halcyons, the large fishing birds of mythology who deplore misfortunes with their compassionate chants, and Xenocrite de Rhodes in Brunck: *Restes des anciens poètes grecs* (1772 - 1776), a book which Chénier used and in which a young girl was apostrophized: "Your hair, still dripping salt water, unfortunate young lady, victim of a shipwreck at sea, Lysidice." For the reading public of the early nineteenth century who had been moved by the drowning in *Paul et Virginie*, the fate of the young Tarentine seemed to express, in its ancient form, eternal human emotions.

The lamentation which begins the poem is reinforced by the repetition of the first word "Pleurez" ("Weep") at the end of the second line. The tone of tragedy is underscored by the invocation to the "gentle" halcyons or kingfishers, legendary birds considered protected by the gods, who are now called upon to witness the tragedy of one who was unprotected. The third line, "Elle a vécu, Myrto, la jeune Tarentine" ("She lived, Myrto, the young Tarentine" [Dimoff, vol. 1, p. 167]), is striking because of Chénier's use of a euphemism ("she lived") to avoid the ancients' expression of evil portent, "she died." Yet the use of a circumlocution to avoid naming the unnamable has the effect of heightening the fate of the young girl. For as Anthony Pugh has remarked with great perspicacity: " 'Elle est morte' would bring before our eyes a corpse; 'elle a vécu' brings on a very subtle picture, a picture of absence. We see, positively, the girl alive: but we know this picture has been wiped out. The positive reality has receded into the distance."[5]

Indeed, Chénier refrained throughout from dwelling too sorrowfully on the details of death. The description of what was to have happened — the young bride was to have been reunited with her lover — unfolds in the imperfect tense with a total absence of any negatives. The imperfect of the verb "devoir" with its overtones of a failed rendezvous injects a subtle note of foreboding on the reference to the songs and flute of the wedding. The suggestion that there is to be a tragedy becomes imminent with the introduction of the word "mais" ("but") and the subsequent change from the imperfect to the present and the use of *enjambement* correspond to the sudden force of the wind:

> Mais, seule sur la proue, invoquant les étoiles,
> Le vent impétueux qui soufflait dans les voiles
> L'enveloppe.

> But, alone on the stem, invoking the stars,
> The impetuous wind which was blowing on the sails
> Envelops her.

(Dimoff, vol. 1, p. 168)

Catastrophe is henceforth inexorable as Chénier achieved a star-
tling effect of rapidity through the repetitions of the pronoun "elle"
("she") and an entire phrase in addition to choppy rhythms suggesting the movements of the sea. The sailors, far away in the distance, give once again the sense of an image that exists but has never
been realized:

> . . . Etonnée, et loin des matelots,
> Elle crie, elle tombe, elle est au sein des flots.
> Elle est au sein des flots, la jeune Tarentine.
> Son beau corps a roulé sous la vague marine.

> . . . Astonished, and far from the sailors,
> She cries, she falls, she is in the bosom of the waves.
> She is in the bosom of the waves, the young Tarentine.
> Her beautiful body has rolled under the ocean wave.
>
> (Dimoff, vol. 1, p. 168)

The repetition of the words "la jeune Tarentine" first seen in line
three creates not only an echo effect but also confers a tone of
somber dignity to the events. *Enjambements*, moreover, alternate
with a series of lines brought to a full stop with a period. These ex-
tremes of rhythm, which first signalled the encroaching danger, now
underscore the finality of the young Tarentine's destiny. The next
six lines describe the actions of the daughters of the Goddess of the
Sea to protect Myrto's body from "monstres dévorants" ("devouring
monsters"), that is, the humans who were unable to spare her from
drowning. The present nymphs who are summoned to place Myrto's
body in a safe place counter the sailors who were absent at the moment tragedy struck. Significantly, the nymphs do not engage in
tearful outbursts as they do Thetis' bidding, yet Chénier's very understatement lends a painful dignity to their task as does the use of a
generic term, "monument," to designate Myrto's tomb.

It is only at the conclusion that the poet, who first invoked the halcyons, reappears. Being a human figure, a member of the race of be-
ings who did not protect Myrto, he addresses the young Tarentine in
the negative terms of unfulfillment, accentuated by the same use of
distinct sentences to mark Myrto's death and by the conditionals
formerly used to describe the bride's wedding dress and hair now
having been replaced by negatives:

Hélas! chez ton amant tu n'es point ramenée.
Tu n'as point revêtu ta robe d'hyménée.
L'or autour de tes bras n'a point serré de noeuds.
Les doux parfums n'ont point coulé sur tes cheveux.

Alas! You are not brought back to your lover.
You have not clothed yourself again in your wedding dress.
The gold around your arms has not tightened knots.
Sweet perfumes have not fallen on your hair.

As one of the fullest expressions of Chénier's sensibility, "La Jeune Tarentine" reveals that the essence of his art was that of suggestion through finely nuanced variations of color. In uniting the musical language of the elegy with the plastic beauty of the idyll, Chénier evoked at once the art of the musician, painter, and sculptor. Endowing material reality with subtly controlled affective values, he pointed beyond Romanticism in this work to the limpid musicality of Baudelaire, Heredia, and Verlaine.

IX "Le Malade" (Love and Lovers)

"Le Malade" is one of Chénier's most admired poems. The hint of disquietude in Chénier's childhood poems of love has been intensified here to the point where death is the sole outcome of unrequited passion. While the poem treats the most extreme form of love as a fatal passion it points to the universality of the anguish that love can engender, for neither the son nor his mother is named but are designated rather in generic terms.

Beginning on a note of imploration, the mother's evoking Apollo's youth, then echoing the description in alluding to her son, has the effect of fusing the identity of the two figures, thus adding greater portent to her son's death. Finally, Chénier's use of directly recorded speech, with the exception of the brief narrative description of the mother's return (lines 122 - 128) intensifies the heightened pitch of emotion inasmuch as the speeches of mother and son alike assume the function of the chorus in Greek tragedy. Excessive sentimentality is diffused, moreover, when the mother shows as much concern for her own plight as that of her son.

In replying, the son concludes "tu n'as plus de fils," ("you no longer have a son") and his repetition of these words (again using the present tense) shows that his death is a supreme reality which will determine all future events, thus making it appear as though death has already occurred. His linking his destiny with his mother's

— "non, tu n'as plus de fils . . . Je te perds" ("No, you no longer have a son . . . I am losing you" [Dimoff, vol. 1, p. 130]) — parallels the interdependence of their lives, defined in the mother's plaint to Apollo.

Amidst his torments, his single understated plea for help signals the desperation of his state and, at the same time, shows Chénier's manipulation of the alexandrine: "Tout me pèse; et me lasse. Aide-moi. Je me meurs," ("Everything weighs on me; and tires me. Help me. I am dying" [Dimoff, vol. 7, p. 130]). Youthful innocence becomes symbolized in the purity of the mother's milk and, in an effort to resist the flow of time and consequently the loss of innocence, the mother offers her breast once again to her son, the futility implied in line fifty-five ("Que ce suc te nourrisse et vienne à ton secours" — "May this juice nourish you and come to your aid" [Dimoff, vol. 1, p. 131]) being opposed by the reality of the ninth line, "Assoupis dans son sein cette fièvre brûlante" ("Allay this burning fever in her breast" [Dimoff, vol. 1, p. 129]).

In the son's response his mistress' land becomes inseparable from his image of the mistress herself. The son's personification of nature assumes a movement from the general ("ô vallons! ô bocage!" — "Oh valleys! Oh thicket!") to the particular, the place of his mistress' dwelling, here invested with divine properties:

> Aux bords de l'Erymanthe!
> Là, ni loups ravisseurs, ni serpents, ni poisons.
> O visage divin! ô fêtes! ô chansons!

> On the banks of the Erymanthe!
> There, neither abducting wolves, nor serpents, nor poisons.
> Oh divine countenance! Oh feasts! Oh songs!
>
> (Dimoff, vol. 1, p. 131)

His description of himself as already dead is now complete, for he apostrophizes the absent woman by asking if she will not come to weep over his tomb, a tone that points to what the Romantics would uphold as one of their central tenets, the ambivalent bitter-sweet feelings elicited by love. This posture is maintained by the mother when she speaks of the salutary effect of disclosing one's suffering.

Chénier achieved a remarkable continuity of tone in this piece inasmuch as both figures maintain a high level of emotion in their discourse, either speaking to each other in plaintive tones or appealing to absent figures invested with divine attributes. The actions of both are a function of their awareness of the corroding effects on the will

by passion. It is the very depths of the despair at the contemplation
of a life quickly ebbing that leads the son to enlist his mother's aid in
seeking out the source of his torment. The physical world he evokes
("cette corbeille . . . nos fruits les plus beaux . . . notre Amour
d'ivoire" — "this basket . . . our finest fruits . . . our ivory Venus"
[Dimoff, vol. 1, p. 133]) all fades before his affective state: "Dis-lui
que je me meurs, que tu n'as plus de fils." ("Tell her that I am dying, that you no longer have a son" [Dimoff, vol. 1, p. 133]). At the
end of the poem, speech has been supplanted by slow, halting movement, and, significantly, it is Daphné whose words conclude the
poem.

The conclusion, in which the girl speaks of her willingness to mar-
ry her erstwhile dying admirer, does not constitute an arbitrary, con-
venient formula but is entirely consistent with the different concepts
of love developed throughout the poem. The absolute, consuming
effects of passion on the son engendered equally strong manifestations of maternal love and filial love, and all three have a positive influence on the girl for whom love, in its extended forms, becomes
the greatest good. "Le Malade" joins the universe of Corneille to
that of Racine. Passion bears within it a fatality, yet vestiges of will
remain to be summoned and send the mother on a mission which,
when successful, saved her son's life.

X "Le Mendiant" (Slaves and Beggars)

Although the manuscript of "Le Mendiant," entrusted to
Latouche, was lost, an outline in prose for this poem was discovered
among Chénier's papers. Written in either 1788 or 1789 in London,
this poem, perhaps more than any other, reveals Chénier's adaptation of eighteenth century attitudes towards the moral values of antiquity. The poem is divided into five main sections: (1) the meeting
between Lycus' daughter and the old man, (2) the beggar, received
at Lycus' banquet, speaks of his former state, (3) Lycus promises to
help the beggar find his family, (4) Lycus speaks of his former
poverty, (5) the recognition scene: Lycus realizes that the stranger is
Cléotas.

A. *Part One*

The first three lines of the poem, containing references to
springtime and "la fille de Lycus, vierge aux cheveux dorés" ("the

daughter of Lycus, a virgin with flaxen hair" [Dimoff, vol. 1, p. 202]), immediately cast an aura of moral righteousness on the events that will be described. The sudden shifting from the idyllic scene to the image of a black phantom wandering in the shadow points to the dominant theme of the poem, the impermanence of worldly goods and the vicissitudes of fortune. As in so many of Chénier's works, childhood is associated with moral virtue, for the young girl is called "nymphe," "belle vierge" and "enfant d'une Déesse" by the stranger, who, moreover, speaks in austere, maxim-like phrases. Chénier's having achieved a homogeneity of speech between the ragged beggar and the opulently garbed Lycus points to the immutable values of justice and honor that bind them together and which transcend their outward appearances.

Chénier's art here is one of understatement and concentration. His physical descriptions constitute moral portraits also, for moral qualities touch all those who surround Lycus. His daughter's servant keeps a "vigilance austère" and has a "visage antique." Virtue, moreover, is regenerative; the girl has inherited her mother's "grâces naïves."

The three characters introduced in the first section, young girl, beggar, and servant, so dissimilar in outward social status, are, nonetheless, seen by their language to possess a common moral outlook. The striking quality of their speeches is the joining of noble, bombastic style with lyrical expressions of feeling. These are Corneillean types for whom virtue and justice, qualities which they feel duty-bound to preserve, constitute permanence, as opposed to constantly evolving material fortunes.

B. *Part Two*

The episode relating to the beggar's arrival at the great hall and the description of the feast, a reconstitution of an ancient scene of hospitality with its perfumed oils, incense, figures of onyx and crystal, is thus less lyrical and more plastic than the first scene. It nonetheless evokes the universal emotions of the first section where the juxtaposition of youth, beauty, and the future with decrepitude, sordidness, and the past had the function of eliciting identification with the beggar's needs.

The rough entrance of the beggar is contrasted at first with the naturalness and civility of Lycus and his daughter. The beggar's speech, however, an invocation of the gods to protect his good fortune, provides an explanation for his hasty intrusion: "Trop de pudeur peut nuire à qui vit de bienfaits." ("Too much modesty can be harmful to those who live off kindnesses" [Dimoff, vol. 1, p. 205]). The beggar's lamentation of his present state in view of his former wealth not only points to the irony of the title as he demonstrates that changes of fortune are beyond man's control, but also effaces all distinctions between himself and the other guests.

C. Part Three

Lycus' response underscores the vicissitudes of fortune inasmuch as he speaks four times of the beggar as "mon hôte," in both senses of the word ("my guest" and "my host"). The influence of two Biblical episodes is seen here, the story of the Good Samaritan and the beatitudes of the Sermon on the Mount, in which poverty is not only exalted but is in addition a reflection of future reward in man's ever-changing physical world ("the last shall be first"). Communion is symbolized in the scenes where all the guests empty their wine cups in praise of Jupiter who has delivered a stranger to them. Chénier's beggar is invested with qualities of probity by his unwillingness to receive without giving (a reminder of another beatitude) and by his identification with the soul. Chénier's art here is one where scenes of expansion (a festive gathering and a projected harvest) alternate with those of introspection (statements of universal moral application such as "L'homme est né pour souffrir. Il est né pour changer." — "Man is born to suffer. He is born to change." [Dimoff, vol. 1, p. 209]).

D. Part Four

Chénier's use of images of nature to depict Lycus' progression from poverty to wealth ("Le fruit des dons de sa bonté prospère" . . . "Qu'une fleur éternelle,/Fille d'une âme pure, en ses traits étincelle. . . ." — "The fruit of the gifts of his kind charity" . . . "May an eternal flower,/Daughter of a pure flower, sparkle in his heart" [Dimoff, vol. 1, p. 210]) underscores the notion that a man whom the gods have favored with virtue ("Dieux, l'homme bienfaisant est votre cher ouvrage" — "Gods, charitable man is your precious work" [Dimoff, vol. 1, p. 210]) possesses treasures which never die but which lie dormant, always ready to germinate once more.

Having wished his benefactor a life of joy, Lycus is horrified to learn from the beggar that Cléotas has suffered extreme reverses and is now poor, languishing, and weak, having neither home nor shelter. The image of a Cléotas "errant et fugitif" ("lost and homeless") is accentuated by the irregular, shifting rhythms of his speech:

> Revêtu de ramée ou de quelques lambeaux,
> Et sans que nul mortel attendri sur ses maux,
> D'un souhait de bonheur le flatte et l'encourage;
> Les torrents et la mer, l'aquilon et l'orage,
> Les corbeaux, et des loups les tristes hurlements,
> Répondant seuls la nuit à ses gémissements . . .

> Clothed in small leaves or in a few rags,
> And without any mortal touched by his misfortunes,
> With a wish of happiness flatters him and encourages him;
> The torrents and the sea, the wind and the storm,
> Ravens and the melancholy howlings of wolves
> Alone responding to his groans in the night . . .

(Dimoff, vol. 1, p. 211)

E.   Conclusion

Recognizing the beggar's seal as the one he had previously given to Cléotas, Lycus perceives the true identity of his guest and expresses shame at his wealth in view of Cléotas' poverty. Relieving the misery of his former benefactor and thus repaying his debt, he gives thanks to his daughter who reunited them. The circularity of men's lives is thus reinforced in the reference at the close of the poem to the young girl described in the opening lines.

Despite Lycus' rehabilitation of Cléotas and the depiction of what Scarfe calls "the paradise of the Golden Age,"[6] the tone of "Le Mendiant" is one of prevailing pessimism. The conditions under which Chénier wrote the poem are all reflected within, his extreme discontent with his situation in London and his dismay at the report of increasing instability in his country's government. The poem's message of the overwhelming impermanence of human affairs because of an unknowable Providence runs deeper than the possibility of ameliorative change. The bliss shared by the three characters at the end becomes a portent of future disasters which, because of the nature of Providence, cannot be foreseen and therefore cannot be checked. That Lycus always comes up with the "right" response does not alter the fact that there is an implicit tone of resignation to the ways of the world in this poem.

"Le Mendiant," even more significantly, reveals the complexity of the bucolics. Although these works represent, more fully than any other, Chénier's absorption with the subjects of the ancients, they suggest, at the same time, his concern with shadings of tone and color, all of which constitute the suggestive nature of poetry, and the wide range of technical skills he could draw upon in order to achieve the desired nuance. As a group, the bucolics are among Chénier's most successful works, poems in which beggars, blind poets, coy lovers, and embodiments of purity who die before their time, in short the material of ancient mythology, are brought down from Parnassus and invested with both aesthetic detail and psychological realism.

CHAPTER 4

The Elegies

ANDRÉ Chénier's elegies are among his most varied poems. It has been seen that when Chénier borrowed subjects from antiquity in the bucolics he not only modified relationships between mythological figures but subordinated plot to tone and color and thus communicated his own vision of the ancient soul. The bucolics reveal Chénier's technical skills and consequently have a particular aesthetic interest. The elegies, which I have treated in four groups following Dimoff's classification — love, friendship, poems related to the Italian journey, and the London elegies — represent a tempering of Chénier's interest in the ancients with the worldly influence of Parisian society.

In ancient times the elegy was a lyric, usually formal in tone and diction, and suggested either by the death of an actual person or by the poet's contemplation of the tragic aspects of life.[1] As a means of countering his melancholy, the poet strove to find consolation in the contemplation of some permanent principle. Poets in France had attempted to copy the elegy form from the ancients by imitating the classic distich (a pair of metrical lines, usually rhymed) in alexandrine couplets and later by alternating decasyllabic lines with octosyllabic lines. By the sixteenth century, Ronsard and others had abandoned the attempt to reproduce the classical meter but returned to the subject matter of the classical elegists.

By the seventeenth century the elegy as a literary genre hardly existed. Boileau, in defining it, had in mind the ancient elegy. Although love was taken seriously in the great works of the century, such as *Phèdre* or *Andromaque*, and the disorders of passion were studied with profundity, the great interest of eighteenth century poetry was not love but gallantry. Since the primary goal of such poetry was to please, it is not surprising that this light verse evoked the boudoir and was sensual, epicurean, and, above all, graceful. At the same time, however, writers such as Diderot and Rousseau in France and foreign authors such as Arthur Young and Gessner called for the restoration of intimate emotions in poetry. Despite the influence of foreign Preromantic elements and the publication of such works as Prévost's *Manon Lescaut* and the rise of the *drame larmoyante*, light poetry, with its frivolous conception of love, was nonetheless still very much alive at the end of the century. Perhaps a psychological reason exists for the preponderance of light, frivolous boudoir poetry in eighteenth century France. Most prose involved somber discussions of religion, society, art, government, nature, and man's destiny. Prose writers, such as Montesquieu, Voltaire, or Diderot, engaged in satire with very serious aims, of course, and poetry of the epigrammatic school consequently provided a respite from the intensely intellectual content of the century's prose. This does not mean that poetry was inherently a less appropriate medium of serious communication in the eighteenth century but rather that a type of poetry flourished under the aegis of relaxed mores with the death of Louis XIV in 1715 which, along with Watteau's *fêtes galantes* and Fragonard's works, provided a counterpart to the pragmatic rationalism fostered by the philosophic party.

André Chénier's elegies reflect a duality, his recognition of the need for inspiration and his deep-seated ties to scholarship and the works of the ancients, his belief that the poet must describe only lived experiences and the immense store of erudition upon which he drew to animate these experiences.

I   *The Love Poems*

If, on the one hand, André Chénier believed that the heart alone gives birth to great poetry, he also espoused in his *Essai* the principle of *naïveté*, by which he meant the expression of a universally felt emotion which would stir the hearts of men. Since this doctrine of universality suggests also a doctrine of impersonality, critics have examined Chénier's early love poetry from the perspective of the poet's sincerity.

Turning to Chénier one finds that the poem written during his adolescent love affairs are of interest not because they record the emotions of hope, jealousy, and despair which are traditionally associated in literature with the lover but because they reveal Chénier's technical skills, his searching for new images to reorchestrate old themes.

II   *"Lycoris"*

The group of seven poems which constitute the "Lycoris" cycle were dedicated to Chénier's first mistress, a young woman believed to be either a singer or a dancer at the Opéra, designated by a name common among both ancient and modern poets. The first poem, written in April, 1782, indicates that love for the eighteen year old poet did not mean anything more than fleeting epicurean delights, the pleasures of physical possession. Significantly, Chénier's mistress is evoked in the language of antiquity: "le cristal . . . Bacchus . . . la ronde . . . ma déesse."

Describing his love as more than intoxication, Chénier concluded by apostrophizing himself as a young man, his alter ego, who has the strength of will that Gallus, seized by love, no longer possesses. Love does not dwell with hate here but, synonymous with life itself, is necessarily linked with death in its most ecstatic moments. Imploring the young man to take him to his beautiful mistress, he invokes an image of consuming love in which it is nonetheless his beloved rather than he who dies.

The vast erudition upon which Chénier could draw gave rise to a melancholy that is clearly distinguishable from the indeterminate ennui of nineteenth century Romanticism. It is a rather that of a pagan epicurean or stoic. The Lycoris elegies hold our attention because of the poet's ability to evoke the ardor of adolescent love against a background of literary conceits.

III   *"L'Art d'aimer"*

At the time that Chénier was involved with "Lycoris" he was also writing an "Art d'aimer" of which fifty fragments survive. While using Ovid's "Art d'aimer" as a guide, Chénier amplified his master's work to include his own psychological observations on the complexities of love. The "Art d'aimer" thus complements the elegies and, at the same time, reveals the state of constant tension between reason and emotion that was a dominant aspect of Chénier's personality. Discussing the duality of human emotions, Denis de Rougemont has concluded: ". . . our human passions are always connected with antagonistic passions, our love with hate, and our pleasures with our pains. . . . It is because passion cannot exist without pain that passion makes our ruin seem desirable to us."[2]

Chénier's point of departure in the "Art d'aimer" was that of the

myth of passion in the Tristan and Iseut legend alluded to by de
Rougemont. A cardinal rule for the lover to remember is the merit of
not constraining one's feelings. What glory can one attain, asks Chénier, what pleasure, in being willfully separated from one's love in
implicit intellectualization processes implied in the very title "Art of
loving." This game is not limited to men, however, for Chénier discussed women who, loving the man who holds them in their arms,
say no with their lips and are at once fearful of giving themselves
and defending themselves. It is no small paradox that in a century in
which Mme du Châtelet, Mme du Deffand, and Mme de Graffigny,
among other women, assumed singular intellectual leadership, the
most ardent male writers should continue to entertain simplistic and
condescending ideas about women. Chénier was very much a man of
his times in this respect. While celebrating the value of not with-
holding one's feelings in matters of love, Chénier went on to conclude that "Une belle est un bien si léger, si mobile!" ("A beautiful
woman is such a light treasure, so mobile" [Dimoff, vol. 2, p. 180]),
that unfaithfulness was natural to women but also that knowledge of
this fact will enable men to at least wage an equal contest.

Although Chénier's portrait of love in the "Art d'aimer" evokes
the boudoir atmosphere of gallant poetry where love, professed to be
serious, was reduced to a frivolous game, his insights into the psychology of love foreshadow Stendhal in the nineteenth century and
Proust in the twentieth. Chénier's awareness of the masochism and
self-destructive impulses involved in love was rare for his century:

> . . . Même sans chercher d'amoureuses promesses . . .
> Vous voulez plaire même à qui vous pláît le moins.
>
> . . . Without seeking pledges of love . . .
> You wish to please the very one whom you please the least.
> (Dimoff, vol. 2, p. 184)

In addition, he made it clear that the mechanisms of love defied intellectual analysis and resided rather in the elusive domain of the
emotions:

> C'est l'amour qui, trompant la sombre vigilance . . .
> En signes inconnus fait parler le silence,
> A l'oeil mobile et prompt sait donner une voix.

It is love which, deceiving somber vigilance . . .
Makes silence speak in unknown signs,
And knows how to give a voice to the prompt and mobile eye.
(Dimoff, vol. 2, p. 192)

Most significantly, however, the numerous mythological allusions and depersonalized language of the "Art d'aimer" evoke the states of alternating hope and despair, of self-mastery and self-effacement, that characterized Chénier's love affairs before he achieved the spiritual love he was to know with Fanny Lecoulteux.

In the remaining poems for Lycoris Chénier's mistress is rarely personalized but is rather depicted as an object which, as Scarfe has noted, enabled Chénier to play at being "the poet in love."[3] These poems are not noteworthy for their themes; their interest lies in their shifting moods. Chénier's erudition surfaces more readily here than does his youth. What strikes our attention is not the desire to possess Lycoris but the absence of any keenly felt happiness in his liaison. These poems reveal the force of imagination in love.

Love, which has spurred the poet to dream, can control his perception of nature and the world. In the fourth elegy, his injunction to his muses to live in other bodies is a vain attempt at exorcism, for he remains haunted by the thought of Lycoris' infidelities. As is typical, the power of love is evoked through the short phrases addressed to Lycoris which punctuate his distress ("J'ai des yeux . . . Je te vois . . . Je suis là" — "I have eyes . . . I see you . . . I am there" [Dimoff, vol. 3, p. 49]), but, as is equally typical in these works, the poem ends on a note of wistful sadness, as he expresses his desire that Lycoris never love him if not of her own volition.

The compelling power of imagination is again the subject of the elegy. Here it is not love that is apostrophized and personified but rather hope, the friend who is far from him. The name of Lycoris is invoked, she who makes his days bitter and who, in the manner of Marot, would have been loved by him unto death. Yet, he does not seek vengeance but rather solitude. This time his flight of imagination turns inward and allows him the comfort of seeing before him an old and dying Lycoris who now asks for his love and the opportunity to please him. Suddenly he emerges from his reverie, painfully aware that reality will provide him no such comfort.

In the seventh elegy, nostalgic sentimentality for a created future has been replaced by recognition of the fact that he is destined to be forever under Lycoris' control. Knowing of her unfaithfulness he returns to her in order to have insults heaped upon him. In vain does he attempt to practice the constraint of the "Art d'aimer." Apostrophizing himself in the form of a "jeune imprudent" ("impetuous young man"), thus suggesting the universality of his plight, he counsels the lover to laugh at his mistress' tears and sighs and to treat her coldly. The gulf between intellect and emotion is nonetheless insurmountable.

The sufferings of love have a bitter-sweet quality about them (the adjective "doux" — "sweet" — is often juxtaposed with the noun "fiel" — "gall") and one does not die of them. His wish to make Lycoris weep by his anger and insults is short-lived, for he is suddenly appeased by the thought of a calm, serene mistress. The "silence indulgent" ("indulgent silence") which he now calls on gives him the moment for reflection and the realization that he can transcend what appears to be a hopeless destiny: "S'il est vrai que la paix soit toute en mon pouvoir ("If it is true that calm is entirely within my power" [Dimoff, vol. 3, p. 61]).

The love poems for Lycoris constitute a period of apprenticeship in Chénier's life in which he attempted to juxtapose worldly codes of behavior with intimate feelings. Lycoris, never idealized, is the object of the poet's erotic desires, yet descriptions of her physical traits are curiously absent.

The expanding-contracting rhythm of this verse, designating the shifting from depersonalization to self-revelation, underscores the antithetical states of emotion depicted by Chénier — hope and despair, anger and tenderness, jealousy and detachment. While the poet desired to possess his unfaithful mistress, the predominant tone of these poems is more cerebral than sensuous and the lover's griefs are more subject to the dictates of a well-established contest than to deep-seated feelings. For example, the poet is offered advice by his confident, a lamp in his mistress' bedroom:

> . . . Suis mon exemple, cesse.
> On aime un autre amant. Aime une autre maîtresse,

> . . . Follow my example, Give up.
> She loves another lover. Love another mistress.

(Dimoff, vol. 3, p. 53)

What emerges here is the impossibility of Chénier's focussing on any instances of shared happiness. The nostalgia that surfaces here is a created nostalgia and the unemotional advice offered the poet, so reminiscent of Letter 141 in Laclos' *Les Liaisons Dangereuses*, does not portend tragedy, despite the suggestion of death in the verb "cesser" (to cease or stop), for the liaison had been sustained solely on negative emotions and its future demise does not point so much to the ephemeral quality of all human actions as to the natural course of a liaison characterized more by desire than fulfillment, more by self-effacement than expansiveness.

IV *The Camille and D'z.n. Cycles*

Between the end of 1784, when André Chénier returned from Switzerland, and his departure for London at the end of 1787, he was involved in intermittent intervals with Mme de Bonneuil, eight years his senior. Mme de Bonneuil, the wife of a very rich old man, was a highly sensitive and cultured woman. According to her son-in-law, the poet Arnault, André Chénier had loved her "to the point of despair."[4] Concluding that it was Mme de Bonneuil, a thirty year old woman, who controlled the course of their liaison, Dimoff states that André Chénier was received in her salon at Sénart on several occasions and that the forests and grottos surrounding the estate were described in the elegies Chénier dedicated to her.[5] Although both Gabriel de Chénier, the poet's nephew, and Becq de Fouquières held that the poems written for D'z.n. and Camille were meant for many different women, it is now believed that both sets of poems were inspired by Mme de Bonneuil and that the D'z.n. poems were composed at the beginning of the liaison.

While not nearly as Machiavellian as Laclos' fictitious creation, Mme de Merteuil, Mme de Bonneuil, like many women of her century, attempted to dissimulate her true feelings in public, which led to a considerable degree of uncertainty on Chénier's part. It was decidedly Mme de Bonneuil who dictated the terms of their relationship. When she departed for Geneva one day, leaving Chénier at Sénart, she asked him to write tender verses for her, but, finding that he was unable to do without her, he wrote: "Camille, où tu n'es point, moi je n'ai pas de Muse" ("Camille, I have no Muse where you are not" [Dimoff, vol. 3, p. 63]).

The reactions of Chénier's friends to the influence of Mme de Bonneuil were fairly consistent. François de Pange ridiculed him for allowing his emotions to gain control over him, Abel de Malartic chastized his friend for wasting his talent, whereas the Trudaines felt that he had kept the same mistress too long. Although Chénier (who broke with Mme de Bonneuil in 1787 and had begun a friendship with Marie Cosway, the beautiful wife of the portrait painter, in the same year experienced pure spiritual love only with Fanny Lecoulteux, he composed the greatest number of love poems for Mme de Bonneuil, many of which were delivered personally to her and have not survived.

The elegies for Mme de Bonneuil constitute portraits of the subjective, contradictory, dreamlike states that are associated with love. Frequently speaking of himself in the third person and putting monologues in the mouths of imaginary persons, a stylistic device that suggests the mind of a man in whom reason and feeling were in perpetual conflict, Chénier revived in these works both the sensualism and sentimentality of the poetry of antiquity. Moreover, the vocabulary he used to evoke his feelings is generally classic; disdain is communicated by "le ris" ("the laugh"), romantic ardor by "le feu" ("fire"), the hope or despair of love is contingent on the way his mistress looks at him ("les yeux" — "eyes" — here are invested with affective quality), the expectation of love linked with blooming flowers ("les roses"), possession by description of her "sein" ("breast"), the haunting thoughts of Mme de Bonneuil by "fantômes" ("phantoms"), and his suffering by "des larmes" ("tears"). Personification of parts of the body, such as Camille's breast, and of inanimate objects is common as are apostrophes to elements in nature, particularly "le vent" ("wind"). It is not in the creation of original images then that Chénier's elegies for Mme de Bonneuil are striking but rather in the depiction of the ever changing states of the lover's soul.

Although the cause of his suffering is always the same — his mistress' departure and unfaithfulness — the suffering itself takes many forms. Suffering in these poems is as important as desire, for it is a function of Chénier's pervading theme, the failure of the will to root out from the lover's memory the object of his love. The antitheses of hope and disappointment, past pleasures and present pain, present infidelities and imagined future contrition, all of which are developed by Chénier in these elegies, are fundamental to his dual nature, in which the attraction to the excitement and accelerated tempos of worldly society is tempered by a need for withdrawal and contemplation. It is this latter quality that surfaces in the D'z.n. and Camille elegies. Anticipating Proust's revelations about the pathological nature of love, especially of the Swann who, years after marrying Odette, could muse with bitterness that he had wasted years of his life for a woman who wasn't even his type, Chénier's thoughts of his beloved do not fill him with a sense of plentitude but rather convey an inescapable sense of solitude. Left only with the resources of his imagination when his mistress had taken flight, Chénier became the chronicler of a fantasized universe. Dreams cannot be sustained, however, and must clash with the world of reality. "The plaint which pours out touches the reader less than the plaint which is divined; the presence less than the absence. . . . In its full furor, feeling fills the soul less than memory and memory less than the dream."[6]

His mistress' indifference is more painful than her insults and thus makes his suffering bitter-sweet. On the other hand, his preoccupation with her has become an obsession. The battle imagery of courtly love is revived ("Contre elle, contre lui je me fais des remparts" — "Against her, against it, I am building ramparts" [Dimoff, vol. 3, p. 83]). But the anticipated call to action becomes a dissipation of the will and all creative impulse ("D'elle seule occupé, mes jours coulent en vain" — "Occupied with her alone, all my days flow in vain" [Dimoff, vol. 3, p. 83]). Bidding farewell to the fine arts he deigns to hope that he is still in D'z.n.'s mind.

One *alliance de mots*, or joining together of two normally opposed elements ("douces impostures" [Dimoff, vol. 3, p. 84]), is a key phrase in the context of these elegies. Love, a microcosm of life itself, courts suffering and, by implication, death, but the calm of not having one's emotions stirred implies a more imminent death.

V The Camille Elegies

The sense of isolation in Chénier was heightened by his frequent use of an interior monologue at the beginning of an elegy, thus creating the impression that the thoughts of the poet reverberated inwardly and that any relief gained by the mental verbalization of his anguish was chimerical. Love in Chénier frequently involved a process of contraction rather than expansion. Whereas Lamartine and other Romantics called on nature in its eternity to witness past happiness, and thus evoked a state of wistful resignation to human mortality, Chénier's references to nature suggested a mood of nervous agitation:

> Absente, je la tiens en des grottes muettes. . . .
> Mais présente, à ses pieds m'attendent les rigueurs,
> Et, pour des songes vains, de réelles douleurs.
> Camille est un besoin dont rien ne me soulage.

> Absent, I possess her in silent grottos. . . .
> But present, hardships await me at her feet,
> And, for vain dreams, real sufferings,
> Camille is a need which nothing assuages.
>
> (Dimoff, vol. 3, p. 62)

Nature was also for Chénier a thick, confined space where the air does not seem to renew itself:

> . . . sonore habitant de la sombre vallée . . .
> Les cieux sont enflammés . . .
> Qu'un berceau de platanes épais
> La mène en cette grotte. . . .
>
> . . . somber inhabitant of the somber valley . . .
> The heavens are ablaze . . .
> May a cradle of thick plane trees
> Lead her to his grotto. . . .
>
> (Dimoff, vol. 3, pp. 62 - 63)

In these poems Chénier became the supreme painter of love as a state of disequilibrium. His portrait of bygone moments when Camille would have preferred death to leaving him serves essentially as a focal point for the effect of her indifference on him. Above all, love produces a degenerative melancholy to the point where periods of respite from pain exist only in the imagination.

This state of agitation is nonetheless preferable to calm:

> Moi, je hais le repos. Quel que soit mon effroi
> De voir de si beaux yeux irrités contre moi,
> Je me plais à nourrir de communes alarmes.
> Je veux pleurer moi-même, ou voir couler ses larmes . . .
>
> I loathe repose. Whatever my fright might be
> In seeing such beautiful eyes incensed against me,
> I am pleased to nurture such common alarms.
> I wish to weep myself or to see tears flow . . .
>
> (Dimoff, vol. 3, p. 68)

In the seventeenth century the Princesse de Clèves followed a conscious path of self-negation when, after her husband's death, she chose to retreat to the calm of the convent and therefore denied her feelings for the Duc de Nemours: "Il est vrai que je sacrifie

beaucoup à un devoir qui ne subsiste que dans mon imagination,"
("It is true that I am sacrificing a great deal to a duty which exists
only in my imagination" Mme de La Fayette, [*La Princesse de
Clèves*, ed. Antoine Adam, (Paris) Garnier-Flammarion, 1966, p.
175]). In his relationship with Camille, on the other hand, Chénier
sought constant stirrings and changing moods in the absence of
which he knew that love, and by extension, life, ebbs. It thus became
necessary to sustain the very feelings about whose obsessive powers
he lamented. Camille's anticipated outburst, described as the lover
approaches her solitary garden, is transformed into a sensuous
universe where physical desire and submission prevail, accentuated
by a striking inversion:

> Ah! le verre et le lin, délicate barrière,
> Laissent voir à nos yeux la tremblante lumière
> Qui, jusqu'à l'aube, au teint moins que le sien vermeil,
> Veille près de sa couche, et garde son sommeil.

> Ah! the glass and the flax, delicate barrier,
> Allow the shimmering light to be seen by our eyes
> Which, until dawn, of a shading less crimson than hers
> Waits near her couch and protects her sleep.

> (Dimoff, vol. 3, p. 70)

Camille overpowers him, leading him to take flight in search of the
peace that is never to be forthcoming:

> Fuyons, vite, courons. Mes projets seront sûrs
> Quand je ne verrai plus sa porte ni ses murs.

> Let us flee, quickly, let us run. My projects will be secure
> When I shall no longer see her door or her walls.

> (Dimoff, vol. 3, p. 70)

Chénier celebrated here not the moment of possession but of an-
ticipation and, by extension, the effect of loss in much the same way
as the Jean-Jacques Rousseau of the *Confessions,* who described in
detail the delights of expectation as opposed to the frustration of
confrontation with a Venetian courtisan. Time is no longer differen-
tiated but becomes an indistinct blur in Chénier's mind as reality
and imagination merge.

That Chénier was torn between the hope of gaining access to
Camille's heart and the desire to achieve the degree of self-mastery

that would enable him to retreat, is seen in the eighth elegy. Once again interior monologue is used at the beginning:

> Non, je ne l'aime plus; un autre la possède.
> On s'accoutume au mal que l'on voit sans remède.

> No, I no longer love her; another possesses her.
> One becomes habituated to the evil which one sees
>   without remedy.

(Dimoff, vol. 3, p. 73)

He cannot reconcile himself, however, to a fate for which he feels unresponsible and, despite his confession of indifference to Camille, recalls his mistress' past promises of retiring to a hamlet far from the city. The simplicity, the total involvement in Camille which such an adventure would involve, in short the lyrical élan which pervades these lines, relates to imagined, rather than experienced, joys and constitutes the essence of love in the poems, an elusive state that alternates between opposing desires, none of which is ever fully realized.

Love here is indistinguishable from hate and embodies a Racinian fatality, a paralyzing of the will for which there is no cure. Submission, pride, and despair have converged and the poet's unwillingness to speak of his new self-mastery indicates that his feelings for Camille are as intense as ever. Even in a state of intoxication he is haunted everywhere by his mistress' name, her absent voice.

In the seventh elegy the poet suggests that the lover, once smitten, is subject to the control of outside forces and, at the same time, that the feelings engendered by love transcend the earthly sphere: "Les amants sont guidés par les Dieux." ("Lovers are guided by the Gods" [Dimoff, vol. 3, p. 72]).

In the closing lines of the cycle the sense of isolation between the lover and the rest of humanity is irremediable:

> Riez, amis; nommez ma fureur insensée.
> Vous n'aimez pas, et j'aime. . . .

> Laugh, friends; call my passion insane.
> You do not love, and I love. . . .

(Dimoff, vol. 3, p. 77)

Submission is no longer comic but painful. The first alternative foreseen by the lover — being pardoned for having loved in vain — can only perpetuate the cycle, whereas the second — death — offers a measure of relief from a debilitating process in which the will can no longer function.

VI *Marie Cosway*

If the elegies for Lycoris revel in pure sensuousness and those for Mme de Bonneuil depict love in terms of obsessions and conflicts, the works written for Marie Cosway speak of this woman in reverent, idealized terms and belong to the tradition epitomized by Rousseau's portrait of Mme de Warens in his *Confessions*. In reading these poems one feels that Chénier loved Marie Cosway with a tender affection, full of respect and deference. Although these poems were written when Chénier was still haunted by his relationship with Mme de Bonneuil, the tone is much closer to the odes for Fanny Lecoulteux than those dedicated to Lycoris and Camille. Married to a much older man, like Mme de Bonneuil, Marie Cosway appears to have been the far more sensitive of the two women.

One of the most striking characteristics of these poems is a lack of self-consciousness. Whereas the Mme. de Bonneuil cycles reveal a poet who was more intent on recording the all-encompassing effects of unrequited love — whether real or imagined — than on focussing on the cause of this degeneration, the later works depict woman as sanctifier, exerting an inspirational influence on admiring men. From the very first lines Marie Cosway became the embodiment of eternally feminine beauty and grace, a woman in whom the most precious offerings of nature were combined in exquisite harmony:

> De l'art de Pyrgotèle élève ingénieux,
> Dont, à l'aide du tour, le fer industrieux . . .
> Sait confier les traits de la jeune Marie,
> Grave sur l'améthyste ou l'onyx étoilé
> Ce que d'elle aujourd'hui les Dieux m'ont révélé.
>
> Ingenious pupil of the art of Pyrgoteles
> Whose industrious iron, with the help of the lathe
> Knows how to commit the features of the young Marie,
> Engrave on amethyst or studded onyx
> What the Gods have today revealed to me of her.
>
> (Dimoff, vol. 3, p. 87)

Whereas the transports of jealousy and uncertainty brought about by Camille resulted in a state of agitation, the apprehension of Marie transcended the world of mundane reality ("L'harmonieux démon descend et m'environne,/ Chante." — "The harmonious demon descends and surrounds me,/ Sings." [Dimoff, vol. 3, p. 87]) but the normally antithetical elements ("harmonieux démon") suggest that, far from being paralyzed by emotions that have gained control over him, the poet will henceforth be able to draw on previously untapped creative resources. Camille's dual nature took form in her unpredictable moods, in which the poet would either be welcomed or repulsed. Marie Cosway reflected for André Chénier a different kind of duality.

She was of a delicacy and purity that distinguished her from other women (her name is after all that of the Virgin), yet, at the same time, her unaffected beauty and grace were associated with nature and suggested her moral virtues even more than her physical charms. Using the Arno River of Marie Cosway's native Florence as the basis of an extended metaphor, Chénier depicted his mistress as one "qui sait voir la beauté, fille de la nature" ("who knows how to see beauty, daughter of nature" [Dimoff, vol. 3, p. 88]) inasmuch as she is surrounded by nature's most accomplished creations.

> . . . des pilliers de nacre entourés de jasmin . . .
> . . . un lit de pervenche et de thym . . .
> . . . ce miel doux et flatteur. . . .
>
> . . . columns of mother of pearl surrounded by jasmin . . .
> . . . a bed of periwinkle and thyme . . .
> . . . this sweet and flattering honey. . . .
>
> (Dimoff, vol. 3, p. 88)

Nature has put in her countenance both passion and a pure soul ("ce feu, cette âme pure" — "this fire, this pure soul" [Dimoff, vol. 3, p. 88]). She is at once of this world, yet transcends the everyday by her numerous virtues. She exerts a sanctifying influence on those given to perverse impulses, yet has strength when the need arises. In another striking juxtaposition Chénier spoke of her "sainte fierté" ("sacred pride"). Whereas Camille was defined in terms of her inconstancy, Marie became the embodiment of exemplary moral qualities.

The dramatic change in modality from the D'z.n. and Camille poems to those written for Marie Cosway testifies at once to the range of Chénier's emotions as well as to the fact that by the end of 1785 the twenty-three year old poet, through increased worldly contacts and intellectual activity, had progressed from the inward self-analysis of the youth engaged in analyzing new emotional experiences to the mature young man who, no longer the egocentric adolescent, was capable of seeking in love an ennobling, rather than a self-destructive, experience. It remained for Fanny Lecoulteux to draw out André Chénier's hitherto unexplored lyrical resources and thus become the subject of some of the most poignant verse ever written in the French language.

VII   *The Italian Elegies*

From early childhood André Chénier was interested in Italy and in Italian literature. At the age of nineteen he was reading Petrarch in the original Italian. His predilection for Italian language and literature, a natural outgrowth of his interest in ancient Greece and Rome, was undoubtedly strengthened during his college years and was part of the general return to antiquity in the latter half of the eighteenth century. The painter David, whom Chénier greatly admired, had initiated his friend in the study of the great Italian masters and it is known that Chénier knew Italian before his departure for Italy, at least well enough to read it and to enjoy writing it.[7] A passage of "L'Invention" on the formation of the neo-Latin languages indicates that Chénier liked the harmony and voluptuous slowness of the Italian language. Moreover, his deep feelings for Marie Cosway, the "daughter of the Arno," undoubtedly intensified his attraction to Italy. Although many periods in André Chénier's life are poorly known, the Italian trip is among the least known. The date of the trip can only be approximated as being sometime in 1786 and 1787. If, on the one hand, Chénier's remarks in the *Essai* on Italian literature are among the most incomplete, a number of elegies inspired by this trip reveal the importance that Chénier placed on Italy in his artistic development:

> Belle encor l'Italie attire l'univers,
> Je puisse au sein des arts vivre et mourir tranquille!

> Still beautiful Italy attracts the universe,
> I can live and die tranquil in the bosom of the arts!
> (Dimoff, vol. 3, p. 9)

An evolution in Chénier's thoughts seems to have occurred during this voyage. Following an extremely worldly existence in fashionable

Parisian society with the Trudaines, the Marquis de Moriolles, and Grimod de la Reynière during the months between his return from Switzerland and his departure for Italy, Chénier no longer brought into his work the brooding self-centeredness of the Mme de Bonneuil and Marie Cosway poems. Thoughts of friendship and the exhilarating prospect of studying Italy's vast art treasures seem to have occupied his mind. If the Italian voyage did not cure him of Mme de Bonneuil, it nonetheless enabled him to resign himself to her fickleness with a maturity that had been hitherto lacking. In short, the trip to Italy marked an evolution in André Chénier's conception of love. The familiar lamentations about unrequited love were here tempered by an enthusiasm that suggests a greater measure of self-mastery.

Earlier Chénier had spoken of the dominant emotional side of his nature:

> Je suis né pour l'amour, j'ai connu ses travaux;
> Mais, certes, sans mesure il m'accable de maux. . . .

> I was born for love, I have known its works;
> But, certainly, it overwhelms me with evils beyond
>   measure. . . .

(Dimoff, vol. 3, p. 106)

The Italian elegies record the constant tension between Chénier's need to find the solitude of intellectual pursuits and the worldly pleasures of the flesh, inseparable from his affective nature which Chénier believed constituted the fabric of great poetry:

> O mon coeur, ô mes sens, laissez-moi respirer.
> Laissez-moi, dans la paix de l'ombre solitaire,
> Travailler à loisir quelque oeuvre noble et fière
> Qui, sur l'amas des temps propre à se maintenir,
> Me recommande aux yeux des âges à venir.
> Mais non! j'implore en vain un repos favorable:
> Je t'appartiens, Amour, Amour inexorable. . . .

> O my heart, oh my senses, allow me to breathe.
> Allow me, in the peace of the solitary shadow,
> To work at leisure on some noble and proud work
> Which, fitting to maintain itself on the heap of time,
> Recommends me to the eyes of future ages.

> But no! I implore in vain an auspicious repose:
> I belong to you, Love, inexorable Love. . . .
>
> (Dimoff, vol. 3, p. 27)

During this period Chénier was too beset by recurring kidney stone attacks and financial worries to lose himself entirely in the company of beautiful women. Contemplating suicide, he found that his attachment to life exceeded his rancor against bitter destiny. Indignation and stoicism converge here, for if man, in Chénier's view, can direct the course of his life, he can do so only within the limitations of an inexorable ebb and flow.

The sensuous side of Chénier's nature cannot be ignored, however. His having determined to seek solace in books is not what he ultimately desires:

> Mais si Plutus revient de s[on] [sic] onde dorée
> Conduire dans mes mains quelque veine égarée;
> A mes gestes, du fond de son appartement,
> Si ma blanche voisine a souri mollement,
> Adieu les grands discours, et le volume antique. . . .

> But if Plutus comes back to his gilded wave
> To lead into my hands some errant humor;
> To my gestures, at the heart of his dwelling,
> If my white cousin has smiled softly,
> Farewell ponderous discourses and the ancient volume. . . .
>
> (Dimoff, vol. 3, pp. 25 - 26)

The concept of love in these elegies transcends the physical possession of the "Art d'aimer." The love relationships constitute a microcosm of human existence and the comfort of friendship lessens the loss of inconstant mistresses. Poetry, viewed in the Lycoris, D'z.n., and Camille cycles as an uninspired reflection of the poet's dejected state, has now become the privileged medium for the expression of his most intimate thoughts:

> Il est bien doux d'avoir dans sa vie innocente
> Une muse naïve et de haines exempte,
> Dont l'honnête candeur ne garde aucun secret . . .

> It is really sweet to have in one's innocent life
> A muse which is naïve and exempt from hatred,
> Whose honest candor keeps no secret . . .
>
> (Dimoff, vol. 3, p. 35)

Italy pitted for Chénier's youthful eyes the eternal creations of antiquity and the Renaissance against the constantly shifting direction
of his own fortune. In a posture very much evocative of Montaigne,
Chénier came to terms with his own adolescent desires to crystallize
time by the realization that change is the keystone of a man's life.
The lover's lamentations have been garbed in a new spirituality in
which the uniqueness of the poet's experiences converge with the
universal elements of civilization. The poet's impulse to retreat is
countered by the discovery that friendship is a potential balm to the
anguish caused by unfaithful women. Yet although the tone of these
works suggests a more profound perception of the philosophical
problem of man's finitude, the overwhelming effect is one of un-
resolved tension. Although his definition of fortune in terms of "la
santé, le repos, les arts, et les amours" ("health, repose, the arts, and
love" [Dimoff, vol. 3, p. 9]) embodied both the cerebral and the affective, Chénier viewed both art and friendship through the eyes of
a sensualist, one for whom the consummate eternal beauty of the
plastic arts stood in opposition to his mistresses' inconstancy and in
whose verse friendship was extolled in terms of the reinforcement it
lent to the poet's passionate temperament.

VIII   *The Epistles*

The titles of André Chénier's epistles are addressed to his college
friends, the Marquis de Brazais, Le Brun, Abel de Malartic, the
Trudaines, and François de Pange. Historically a poem addressed to
a particular patron or friend, written in a familiar style, the verse
epistle generally was of two types, one on moral and philosophical
subjects which stems from Horace's *Epistles* and the other on
romantic and sentimental subjects which stems from Ovid's
Heroides.[8]

In several respects Chénier's epistles, written from the late 1770's
to the 1790's, constitute a summation of his thought. They are of major importance inasmuch as they amplify many of the themes of the
poetics, in particular the *Essai* and "La République des Lettres." In
expounding on such philosophical and sentimental subjects as the
mission of the poet, the universality of the primary passions, the
relationship between talent and virtue, and the postulation of an
idealized rustic retreat admittedly antithetical to his innermost
needs, Chénier enlarged the verse epistle far beyond the limits of a
mere enumeration of his friends' qualities.

Chénier saw his early desire for independence, his need to lose himself within the confines of his artistic haven, as a major factor in his poetic vocation. Disclaiming that he had any masters in the art of writing verse he attributed his creative impulse to the duality of his nature, his penchant for introspection, by which he meant the artist's secretly descending into himself to contemplate a perfect model, and his inability to sustain long periods of solitude. He clearly envisaged himself as embracing the discipline of a theoretician such as Boileau, while sharing Voltaire's worldliness and Rousseau's sensibility. To these qualities, however, he added an implicit moral standard which is perhaps the most consistent aspect of his work.

Love for Chénier was not a game whose rules were drawn up in the salon but rather an innately felt emotion whose expression could not be curbed and which in fact inspired his Muse. If Chénier considered his emotional resources dominant over his intellect and could speak with disdain of the ennui of study, he, nonetheless, saw his principal contribution to the arts as a function of his being a new *pontife* (the very word suggests a sacred mission) who, by virtue of his erudition and immersion in his century, could blend French chants with Greek choruses. For all his claims of being indifferent to artistic immortality, he was very much concerned with his reputation. This theory is borne out by his consistently acting as his most severe critic, thus refusing to allow his poetry to appear in print, and by his fantasy of being mourned at his death by many friends.

The friends from the Collège de Navarre and from his mother's salon to whom Chénier dedicated these epistles occupy a special place in his life inasmuch as they alone were granted the privilege of sharing his most intimate artistic aspirations. The fact that some of Chénier's works came before the public more than a century after his death makes the singularity of these friendships all the more apparent. The link between talent and virtue, developed at length in the *Essai*, is a fundamental precept of the epistles. Calling his friends quasi-gods, Chénier viewed friendship as proof of one's superior capacity to feel and to experience the nobler passions, banishing hate and envy from its domain. He believed that he shared with his friends a transcendence of souls reminiscent of Rousseau and founded on mutually shared ideals of virtue.

Love, friendship, and the sublime harmony of the poet's craft all emanated in Chénier's view from the same genius and all were virtues of a great and powerful soul. The vision of an enchanted lake and the simplicity of a rustic life where domestic bliss reigned supreme were contrasted with the perpetual uncertainties of his current romantic involvements. Chénier, nonetheless, acceded to the turbulent course of his emotions with a sense of inevitability.

Destiny, Chénier believed, has decreed that sooner or later all men must love. Chénier's epicureanism is distinguished by qualitative, as opposed to quantitative, concerns. In contrast to the doctrine of Don Juanism developed by Camus in *Le Mythe de Sisyphe*, Chénier did not preach a doctrine of multiplicity as a means of countering man's mortality. His defense of an intensely lived life did not constitute a belief in the individual's ability to achieve ultimate control of his life but was rather a conviction that life, as opposed to existence, is to be defined in terms of passions and feelings.

As an outgrowth of Chénier's epicureanism, the epistles are both sensual and sentimental. Reason, which serves as the basis for universal truths, and lyricism, by which the poet's particular vision is translated, are blended. Like Boileau, Chénier believed that thought and expression were simultaneous and therefore painted his feelings with a plasticity. He also shared Goethe's belief that reality must furnish the subject matter of poetry. The true poet can hope to near perfection in his creation only insofar as his work has nature for its source. Chénier saw in love and friendship man's most primary instincts. The overwhelming sentiment which emerges from these works, however, is one of solitude and suggests once again the tension which existed in him between the worldly poet who celebrated his friends' virtues and the eternal poet who, like the ancients, had to look within himself to discover that he was possessed by an inner voice. Love in the epistles is still physical possession but its meaning has been extended beyond momentary desire. Its essential elusiveness has become synonymous with human destiny itself just as the rose, the symbol most often used by Chénier in speaking of his mistress' lips and cheeks, is the eternal embodiment of a transient beauty.

IX *André Chénier's London Experiences*

The writings prompted by André Chénier's experiences in London from 1787 to 1790 reveal some of the most intimate facets of his personality and provide a lively portrait of English life on the eve of the Revolution. The circumstances surrounding the poet's departure for England in 1787 were not happy ones. His father's multivolume work on the Moors did not have the anticipated favorable results. Financial embarrassment was not something new to Louis Chénier but at this stage in his life, after having lived apart from his family for several years in an effort to improve his fortune, his inability to provide for his wife and the three children who lived with him must have been a crushing blow. More than any other factor it was his father's financial plight that forced André Chénier to take a post at the embassy in London. During his college days and continuing into the 1780's he had relied on the benevolence of such steadfast friends as the Trudaines and François de Pange when health and monetary crises had struck. Now he himself was forced, in the face of his father's dwindling pension, to be an active means of support for his family. The exact circumstances of André Chénier's introduction to his employer at the embassy, a Monsieur de la Luzerne, are not known but it seems reasonable to assume that he was introduced to de la Luzerne by Mme de Beaumont, the ambassador's sister-in-law.

The French Embassy in London was situated in a house on Portman Square and it was here that Chénier had an apartment with François Barthélemy, the nephew of the famous priest. Chénier's work at the embassy was largely unstructured. He principally filled the role of private secretary and although the nature of his work gave him periods of leisure time to see London landmarks, his daily existence frustrated his poetic aspirations.

Chénier's distress in London was caused by a pervading sense of moral isolation. Anglomania among the French in the eighteenth century, nurtured by such authors as Montesquieu and Voltaire, reached its height in the late 1780's. Chénier had himself praised the English model of government in early works, but now, living as a foreigner in London, he was quick to point out English shortcomings. It appears that his sense of humiliation was not the result of excessive cruelty on the part of the English but can be attributed rather to his physical isolation from France, the hiatus in his progress on the didactic poems because of his duties at the embassy, and finally his failure to find among the wealthy of England those who, like the Trudaines and other college friends, made no distinctions of class or wealth. According to the testimony of Barthélemy, Chénier's intelligence and character inspired respect in M. de la Luzerne, whereas Barthélemy and Chénier had similar political views and intellectual affinities.

From Chénier's vantage point the English were guilty of snobbery and superficiality. Speaking of his chagrin in living in an environment where wealth and birth alone were respected, he drew upon

his last resources of pride in an effort to surmount his feelings of rejection; the lines written in Hood's Tavern convey his frustration:

Je sais bien qu'il ne m'arrive rien dont mon honneur puisse être blessé; je
sais bien aussi que rien de pareil ne m'arrivera jamais, car cette assurance-là
ne dépend que de moi seul. Mais il est dur de se voir négligé, de n'être point
admis dans telle société qui se croit au-dessus de vous; il est dur de recevoir,
sinon des dédains, au moins des politesses hautaines; il est dur de sentir . . .
Quoi? qu'on est au-dessous de quelqu'un? — Non; mais il y a quelqu'un qui
s'imagine que vous êtes au-dessous de lui.

I know well that nothing can happen to me to injure my honor. I know well
also that nothing similar will ever happen to me because this assurance de-
pends on me alone. But it is hard to see oneself neglected, not to be admitted in a society which believes itself above you; it is hard to receive, if not
disdain, at least haughty politeness. It is hard to feel . . . What? that one is
inferior to someone? — No, but there is someone who imagines that you are
inferior to him.

                                              (Scarfe, *Chenier . . . Life*, p. 80)

The elegies written during this period are characterized by two
opposing moods, a bitter denunciation of the suffering brought by
cruel destiny alternating with a resolute determination to cheat
death at all costs. This duality, which took the form of Chénier's
refusal to accept his own conclusions on the worthlessness of life, was
typical of his century; Voltaire's *contes* abound in examples of men
relying on projected ideals in order to ward off total despair. For
Chénier the idea of communal suffering made his own circumstances less threatening. Only the thought of remaining alive in his
friends' memories consoled him as he contemplated physical death.
Once again he dreamed of evading the miseries of urban London in
a rustic setting where his remains will serve to remind the traveller of
his unfortunate destiny. Apostrophizing his tombstone he evoked a
picture of simple virtues in which his qualities — disdain for
violence and honesty — serve to heighten the injustice of his death.
He will rest more peacefully if he knows that his friends' thoughts
are full of his memories. Bitterness gives way to compassion as the
inequities of a fate beyond man's control are tempered by thoughts
of lasting emotional ties with friends.

Chénier arrests the reader's attention by continually alternating
his focus. Physical disintegration coexists here with the immortality
of remaining in friends' memories:

Je meurs. Avant le soir j'ai fini ma journée.
A peine ouverte au jour, ma rose s'est fanée.
La vie eut bien pour moi de volages douceurs;
Je les goûtais à peine, et voilà que je meurs.
Mais, oh! que mollement reposera ma cendre,
Si parfois un penchant impérieux et tendre
Vous guidant vers la tombe où je suis endormi,
Vos yeux en approchant pensent voir leur ami!

I am dying. I have finished my day before the evening.
Hardly opened to the daylight, my rose has faded.
Life really had fickle sweetnesses for me;
I hardly tasted them and here I am dying.
But oh! how softly my ashes will rest,
If sometimes an imperious and tender penchant
Guiding you towards the tomb where I am asleep,
Your eyes in approaching think they see their friend!

(Dimoff, vol. 3, pp. 7 - 8)

Reference to the greatest reward that a man can reap in death, however, is reserved for the closing lines in the image of a desolate mistress for whom the thought of continuing without her lover is unbearable.

Chénier's years in London, his first and only attempt to earn a livelihood before engaging in the political journalism of the 1790's, proved to be a period of introspection, of somber self-consciousness rather than worldliness. The overwhelming mood of these elegies and confessional pieces in prose is one of solitude. Insecure among foreigners whose haughtiness he no doubt exaggerated, Chénier clearly rejected the orthodox belief in the immortality of the soul and substituted in its place an imagined rekindling of the memory of the deceased through the thoughts of cherished friends. To the compassion of his friends Chénier opposed the class consciousness of British society, a frame of reference which explains not only his being receptive to the earliest designs of the Revolution but also his later antipathy to the Revolution when he saw it destroying the conditions essential for maintaining a balance between the life of the mind and the life of the heart.

CHAPTER 5

André Chénier and the French Revolution

I André Chénier and French Society

ANDRÉ Chénier's roots were bourgeois. On his father's side he came of an undistinguished bourgeois family that had long been connected with Carcassonne and Limoux. His great-grandfather served in Louis XIV's navy and had flourished in Carcassonne as an attorney to the extent of being appointed as a "secrétaire du Roi" or civil servant. He was the first in his family to call himself "de Chénier" but he died in 1702 before receiving titles of nobility.

On his maternal side Chénier was descended from Levantine Roman Catholics. His grandfather, who acquired considerable wealth by buying and selling jewels, was a man of rich erudition and noteworthy accomplishment. Elisabeth Lomaca, André's mother, had aspirations to having an aristocratic salon but was unable to achieve this end because of her limited financial resources. She was nonetheless able to attract some members of fashionable Parisian society by arranging sumptuous evenings. She therefore resorted to cultivating an intellectual milieu and was remarkably successful in drawing to her salon such notables as the painters David and Cazes.

André's friendship with the Trudaine brothers, the Marquis de Brazais, François de Pange, and Abel de Malartic coincided with his frequenting his mother's salon during the years he attended the Collège de Navarre. To all of them, in particular the Trudaines, Chénier was indebted for moral support and financial aid. Although Chénier was to complain bitterly about the indignations he had to endure in London as a result of his lowly station, he never harbored any resentment toward his aristocratic friends or expressed a desire to rid them of their fortunes and the privileges that accompanied wealth. In fact, it would not be an exaggeration to say that he imbibed their attitudes almost completely and, while in their company, felt completely at one with them. Because of his college friendships André Chénier identified more with the aristocracy than with the bourgeoisie, notwithstanding his frequent financial plights. That is why, like his liberal aristocratic friends and like most of the *philosophes*, moreover, Chénier, knowing the corrupt character of the Ancien Régime, nonetheless felt that an enlightened monarch could institute reform and naïvely believed that Louis XVI was such a person. His friends similarly envisaged a new system modeled on the constitutional English monarchy. As an admirer of Montesquieu, Chénier looked on England as the country of liberty.

Henry Freeman has astutely remarked that one of the most persistent common denominators of eighteenth century thought was the search for a more rational order of society and that nothing could be more irrational than a violent revolution.[1] Advocating reform, Chénier nonetheless objected vigorously to measures he deemed violent and a threat to the existing order, a philosophy which explains much of his opposition to revolutionary doctrines after 1791.

Chénier's views on government and society were shaped not only by his personal associations, his readings of the *philosophes* such as Montesquieu, Voltaire, Rousseau, Condorcet, and Condillac, and his personal observations of the English system of government but by American influences as well. Benjamin Franklin, a celebrated figure in Paris, played a major role in enlisting sympathy for the American cause, whereas Turgot painted America as "the hope of the human race," a country on whose soil the new theories could be put into practice.[2] Chénier and many of his young friends looked at England with decidedly less enthusiasm after the outbreak of the American War of Independence. It seems to me, however, that although America provided an exotic far-off tableau on which Chénier could draw material for an epic poem which did not directly affect his life, it was another matter in view of his associations, readings, and political philosophy, to support a revolution on his native soil that aimed at reconstituting that social order. Moreover, as Walter has pointed out, André Chénier, absent from Paris, was completely unfamiliar with the political rivalries and cabals that were forming on the eve of the Revolution.[3] It was therefore only after he had been back in Paris for some time that he became aware of the various factions that were vying for control of the government.

Two poems written during the 1780's before his departure for London suggest that Chénier's social consciousness was awakened long before the Revolution. In "La Liberté" Chénier evoked in the form of a dialogue a contrast between the goatherd who is happy because he is free and a shepherd who is miserable because he is a slave. In merging an eighteenth century concept with that of antiquity Chénier avoided a simplistic, one-dimensional approach to the subject. Slavery is depicted as the worst of evils precisely because it has such a dehumanizing effect. When asked by the goatherd if he can at least take pleasure in love, the slave replies that women avoid him because he can offer them no gifts ("La Liberté," Dimoff, vol. 1, p. 191). Virtue, moreover, can thrive only in liberty. The slave is a churlish man who wishes to make his dog feel as unhappy as he does. At the end the goatherd, expressing his sympathy for the slave, gives him a gift of a nanny goat and her two kids only to be cursed by the slave who, nonetheless, takes the gift ("La Liberté," Dimoff, vol 1, p. 191). Chénier suggests here that the lack of fundamental natural rights has effects more devastating than immediate economic implications. His shepherd walks the same countryside paths as those of the free man but has been reduced to a vindictive, humiliated person who is in no way capable of contributing to society. Chénier affirmed here, in the manner of Rousseau, the need to free man in order to improve him.

A prose draft of the "Hymne à la justice" reveals Chénier's sympathy for the lowliest peasants' lot: "I have seen beggars in villages . . . the image of misery . . . peasants trampled at the feet of the great, discouraged . . . salt taxes, forced labor, extorters, a thousand ruffians decked with the holy name of prince saddening a province and arguing over its brokenhearted members" ("Hymne à la justice," Dimoff, vol. 2, p. 253).

In the verse form Chénier stated that France has been blessed by nature with a temperate climate, majestic forests, a complex network of winding rivers, and delicious wines that are ripened along her riverbanks. Her people are valient, "born for battle" and have chased away the "impious English." In an imploring tone, however, Chénier begged the French to take advantage of their natural gifts. The English, in his view, who have had the courage to submit their laws to a free and wise governing body, have far surpassed the French. In a moving passage he asked his apostrophized country:

> . . . O combien tes collines
> Tressailliraient de voir réparer tes ruines,
> Et pour la liberté donneraient sans regrets
> Et leur vin et leur huile et leur belles forêts.

O how much your hills
Would thrill to see your ruins restored,
And without regret would give in order to be free,
Their wine and their oil and their beautiful forests!
("Hymne à la justice," Dimoff, vol. 2, pp. 255 - 256)

That this poem is not an inflammatory call to violence is seen in the words: "Ah! si de telles mains, justement souveraines,/ Toujours de cet empire avaient tenu les rênes!" ("Ah, if such hands [those of Malesherbes and Turgot] rightly sovereign/ Still had held the reins of this empire!" ("Hymne à la justice," Dimoff, vol. 2, p. 256 - 257). Chénier's hope for France lay, as these lines show, in the work of enlightened ministers within the framework of constitutional government, a position to which he remained steadfast during the Revolution. The poem ends with an invocation to sacred justice, ignored "for too long on our sad soil," and with the hope that the sweet name of virtue and liberty will once again be heard in his country ("Hymne à la justice," Dimoff, vol. 2, pp. 257 - 258).

It is clear that at the writing of this poem in 1787, Chénier was very much aware of the extent of corruption in his government and the inequities that threatened the very fiber of society. Far from advocating an upheaval of the social order, he expressed his desire to see reforms effected along established traditions. For all his dissatisfaction with present conditions he never suggested for one instant the overthrow of the monarchy, nor did he, in an effort to gain support for his beliefs in the form of a political movement, consent to have this poem published. It is essential therefore to note that Chénier was much more conservative in his political thinking than a few phrases taken out of context from the "Hymne à la justice" might lead one to believe.

II *Chénier and the Revolution*

Between August, 1790, and his death on July 25, 1794, André Chénier published some twenty-seven articles and wrote eight others that were published posthumously. In addition, he published during this period the only two poems that appeared during his lifetime and wrote numerous *iambes*. I have attempted to highlight the major stages of Chénier's political development while showing that the poet and the political analyst cannot be considered independently of one another. I have organized this section around two major headings: (1) Chénier's entrance into politics: from the

"Avis au peuple français" to "Réflexions sur l'esprit de parti" and
(2) Chénier and the Monarchy.

A. *Entrance into Politics*

For some time before his return to Paris in the summer of 1790
André Chénier had accepted an invitation to join in absentia the
Société de 1789, a group that arose from the liberal salons that were
so prevalent in the last half of the eighteenth century. The Société
de 1789, in the manifesto of April 12, 1790, described itself as
"neither a sect nor a party but a business company of agents of social
truths." In describing it as "dedicated to the defense of the principles of a free constitution and to the perfection of social art," Condorcet, its first spokesman, pointedly aimed at distinguishing it from
the Jacobins' "Friends of the Constitution" which Chénier's friends
considered decidedly less free. The Société de 1789 came into
prominence when attention was turned to constitutional and ad-
ministrative problems. It was first and foremost a type of political
academy which, seeking to confine its activities to the discussion of
principles, had little desire to get involved with party struggles. Chénier's involvement with the group, which initially counted among its
ranks La Fayette, Mirabeau, Bailly, the Trudaines, the de Panges,
and Abel de Malartic, as well as such future Jacobins as David and
Collot-d'Herbois, typifies his sincere if increasingly naïve desire to
remain independent. The very formation of political clubs, as Walter
has observed, responded to the need to make political homogeneity
out of the chaos that resulted from the mounting impetus to destroy
the foundations of the Ancien Régime.[4]
    It was through the auspices of the *Journal de la Société de 1789*
that Chénier published on August 24, 1790, his first political article,
"Avis au peuple français sur ses véritables ennemis" ("Advice to the
French People on its Veritable Enemies").
    Although Chénier undoubtedly wrote more inspired political arti-
cles, the "Avis" is of capital importance because it revealed the
political posture to which he adhered throughout the first year of the
Revolution. In addition, it marks the first Chénier publication in
either poetry or prose, for although the ode entitled "Le Jeu de
Paume" antedates this article, it was not published until 1791.
    Chénier's first words are striking. His referring to a "just and
legitimate insurrection" showed that although he was aware of the
tyrannical nature of the Ancien Régime he nonetheless viewed recent political events as being of definitely limited duration. The

idealistic strain of Chénier's political thinking is suggested by the adjectives "just and legitimate," whereby he proclaimed his belief that justice will impose itself by a legality before which everyone would bend.

From the start, Chénier's prose bore the influence of Pascal and Rousseau, both of whom used antithesis extremely effectively in their efforts to persuade their readers by the eloquence of their rhetoric. Admitting that the current mass confusion which characterized French politics was a natural consequence of the dissolution of the established order (in addition to the Tennis Court Oath and the Fall of the Bastille, the formulation of the Civil Constitution of the Clergy as well as the uprising of the Swiss mercenaries at Châteauvieux had occurred by the writing of this essay), Chénier went on to chide the leaders of the "insurgents" for not having carried their efforts far enough since all these incomplete reforms were not of a general interest for the multitude. What he proceeded to argue, however, was that the events of 1789 are inconsonant with the civilizing elements that have characterized European governments for centuries. Thus, while claiming to support the recent insurrection, Chénier found more to attack than to praise.

Drawing a very nuanced line between anger and containment, Chénier adopted a stance in which he described and attacked what were obviously his interpretations of contemporary political changes in France but softened his attack by couching his vocabulary in general terms, thereby suggesting that the principles to which he adhered have merit by virtue of their universal applicability. This tension between the universal and the particular was the hallmark of Chénier's rhetoric. After his introduction, in which he concluded that the public weal is in a dangerous state, he went on to identify those whom he deemed responsible for this state ("Avis," Pléiade, p. 206).

Again he adopted the technique of seemingly mitigating particular guilt by sensing widespread general duplicity. It is clear, nevertheless, that Chénier wished to refrain from producing an emotional effect on his readers when he depicted reason and moderation as the predominant states of human behavior. Despite all evidence to the contrary which he himself cited, Chénier did not believe that the current breakdown of order in France was of long-term consequence, and therefore contrasted the excesses of the partisan factions with the return to reason and moderation which he believed to be imminent.

Throughout he adopted a middle course and did not limit his

criticism to one group. Sounding a distinctly modern note, Chénier asserted that patriotism comes in many forms and cannot be imposed as an objective truth. Arguing in a spirit that points to the mood of the United States in the 1960's, Chénier viewed laws and the right to dissent as two ingredients of a free society, one in which public order and private well-being are inextricably linked, for public order founded on respect toward others can come about only when individuals are given enough freedom to respect themselves and to transfer this feeling of well-being to communal institutions. Similarly, laws must reflect the general welfare of those for whom they have been formulated. Thus, Chénier's ideal society resembled that outlined by Rousseau in *Du Contrat Social*.

While denying that France has a unique mission to fulfill and stressing rather the interrelationship of the European communities, Chénier did see naturally favorable conditions in France, specifically her large population and her ability to defend herself. Again, Chénier pointed to the twentieth century when, without suggesting that France place herself in a position of being unable to defend herself militarily, he concluded that the general welfare could be maintained only in peace. Acknowledging that he might be criticized for hinting at social perfection to come when there is such rampant disorder in reality, Chénier considered the law in terms of constant evolution and the ideal law as one which allows the greatest degree of flexibility in order to serve human needs in specific situations.

Chénier saw the breakdown of order in France in terms of a contagious virus which would spread throughout Europe. In this he revealed himself to be an astute political analyst. The destiny of Europe rested, in his opinion, in the hands of France. It is clear that Chénier, like Montesquieu and Voltaire, wished to effect reforms within the framework of constitutional monarchy. France had become, in his eyes, a great testing ground which, if successful in its experiments, would inspire the kings of other European governments to come to terms with their constituents. Unlike Rousseau, however, who did not live to see the Revolution and who, moreover, spoke of society in terms of mythical stages of development which did not correspond to historical realities, Chénier focussed initially on general, abstract political theory in order to express more convincingly his views on the particular problems facing France. Asserting that liberty is derived from a respect for the law on the part of all citizens, he then went on to sum up his argument in favor of orderly government based upon the principles outlined in the Declaration of the Rights of Man: "The wicked are powerful only because of the ignorance of those who listen to them" ("Avis," Pléiade, p. 217). Pointing ahead one hundred and fifty years to the aftermath of World War II in Germany, Chénier made a tenuous distinction between those who originated and enforced tyranny and those who were merely swayed by the eloquence of self-seekers. His aim, he stated, had been to convince the great mass of people that the source of their happiness lay within their own actions. In a closing note which might have been borrowed from La Rochefoucauld, Chénier stated that it is human nature to greet openly those who give full rein to our passions, whereas we do not wish to hear those who utter the voice of reason which might restrict our passions. His method is apparent here; his approach to political theory was motivated by the concerns of a moralist.

Despire Chénier's appeal to reason by his linking personal happiness with public order this essay was interpreted by Desmoulins, among others, and correctly so, as a thinly veiled diatribe against the "patriotic clubs." Predictably, the essay was received with praise by those who shunned the more extreme course of the Jacobins and the clubs which originated from within their body. The Polish king, Stanislas, was so taken with the essay that he had it translated into Polish.

The revolutionary mechanism which was to lead to the Reign of Terror was already in motion. The transfer of the king to Versailles had already been accomplished. Such was the tenor of events at the writing of this article that one month later Necker was to resign as chief minister. André Chénier's inauguration into the world of political journalism did not formally begin with the writing of the "Avis" for he had touched upon the notion of liberty in the "Ode au Jeu de Paume" and of course in the "Hymne à la justice" and "La Liberté." Yet the "Avis" is a noteworthy moment in Chénier's career. Not being able or willing to accept the implications of the rampant anarchy which was spreading throughout France, Chénier unleashed in this essay a tone of exasperation and indignation which was only slightly lessened by the detachment inherent in his stance of the Old Testament moralist-prophet who wished to guide the errant flock into the fold. The mood of France was already one of great elation as a result of the visible spectacle of a civilization undergoing tremendously rapid changes. The spectre of anarchy that was to occur in the next two years occasioned increasingly vocal outbursts by Chénier, which was to result in a more marked separation between himself and the ruling parties. Henry Freeman has stated that many of those who survived the Revolution were able to do so by modifying their position as the course of the conflict changed.[5] André Chénier's unwavering adherence to principles which he believed fundamental to the cause of justice foreshadows his disinclination to "move with the times" and suggests that his approach to politics would be more tempered by the concerns of a moralist than those of a pragmatist. Many members of the Société de 1789, including Chénier's brother, Marie-Joseph, broke ranks with the group lest they be considered among the enemies of the Revolution. After the publication of this article Chénier's name traveled by word of mouth to the cultural milieux of the capital. His political career was definitely launched, for he was now either singled out with praise or denounced as in the case of Camille Desmoulins, for having written an unprecedented attack against patriotic writers.

1. *"Réflexions sur l'esprit de parti"*

A short time after his initial venture into political journalism Chénier went back to London, returning to Paris in April, 1791. His second major article, "Réflexions sur l'esprit de parti," ("Thoughts on Partisan Mentality") was dated March 3, 1791, in the form of a brochure. This essay, written at a time of increased emigration and flow of capital from France, with a corresponding increase of illegal acts against all personal freedoms by the more impassioned revolutionaries, marked a more fervent and angry plea for the restoration of principles outlined in the "Avis." It revealed, moreover, that Chénier continued to remain independent of political factions and that, at this point in the Revolution, his attack was directed more against the violation of principles than against specific individuals. Scarfe has observed in this article "a stiffening of his attitude towards both Right and Left."[6]

Many of Chénier's ideas in this article constitute an amplification of those found in the "Avis." Typically, he founded his arguments on antithesis. Principles must take precedence over momentary popular outcries. Political clubs should conduct open debates instead of fanatically weeding out the opposition. Chénier suggested here the Orwellian character that revolutions invariably assume, the fact that they begin as ideals and end as businesses.

Calling for the establishment of principles in the French government that would allow just elections to the National Assembly and allow them to be recognized as such by the people, Chénier, the student of sociological principles and principles of cultural relativism in his lengthy *Essai* and other works, here affirmed his belief that "fruitful human principles" are eternal and know no barrier of time and space ("Réflexions," Pléiade, p. 237). These values were cited as diametrically opposed to the *honneur de corps* (collective honor) adopted by so many who, having abdicated personal honor, find it much easier to hide their shortcomings in the name of public weal. This so-called "collective honor," the other side of the "collective guilt" depicted by Albert Camus in *La Chute*, has, in Chénier's opinion, made men implacable enemies of their country who rejoice in bloodshed, falsifying decrees, and spreading seeds of discord. In this passage Chénier revealed one of the attitudes that most persistently influenced his politics, his endemic fear of mob psychology and mob rule.

Although Chénier would in later articles affirm his belief in the right of priests to dissent, he attacked here what he considered the political and economic motivations of those priests who wished to remain independent of Rome. In keeping with his policy of attempting to transcend factional politics which attach more importance to labels than to principles, Chénier then chided both radical and royalist groups who, in proscribing the use of the word "Republic," had prided themselves on ridding France of à sacrilege, an enemy of the state of the king.

The last section of the essay, dealing with Edmund Burke's *Reflections on the French Revolution*, was prompted by the contemptuous comment in Burke's work on Marie-Joseph Chénier's play *Charles IX*. Chénier concluded his essay by addressing a citation to Burke, this "arrogant sophist, an orator without discretion or measure whose head was filled only with unworthy and inexhaustible inanities" ("Réflexions," Pléiade, p. 246). Thus did Chénier demonstrate his loyalty to a brother who most often did not respond in kind.

In a tortuous, convoluted manner reminiscent of Montaigne, Chénier appears to have arrived at his *raison d'être* only at the conclusion of the essay. Within the body of this work, however, he exhibited the line of thought that would be intensified in his later writings, a fear of the influence of groups and mob psychology and, paradoxically, an inherent aversion to the behavioral characteristics on which he believed political success was traditionally founded — hypocrisy and an appeal to the emotional instincts of the masses.

2. "Ode au Jeu de Paume"

Chénier's very conception of the "Ode au Jeu de Paume" is itself revelatory of the ambiguous position he occupied during the Revolution, for this, the first poem he ever saw in print, was published in 1791 by Bleuet, an editor known for his right-wing propaganda. The original manuscript has been lost but it is known that in June, 1790, the Jacobins held a banquet during which it was proposed that a subscription be raised to enable Chénier's friend, the painter Louis David, to commemorate the Tennis Court Oath by painting an enormous scene in which all the deputies present on that historic occasion would be portrayed.

In condemning in his "Avis" the excesses which had marked the course of the Revolution, Chénier spoke in favor of reason and the application of moderate principles which would form the foundation of a viable, constitutional government. There is no doubt that those who would later be in the forefront of the movement to dissolve the French monarchy and behead Louis XVI would be receptive to the very idea of a poem which celebrated an act of civil disobedience. Yet, if in the first part of the poem Chénier celebrated the expression of freedom which he believed underlay the events surrounding the Tennis Court Oath, in the second section of the poem he warned the people against the abuse of power in the name of liberty. Like the painter David to whom he dedicated the poem, Chénier was struck by the spirit which engendered the Tennis Court Oath, but, unlike David, who aligned himself more and more with the excesses of the Jacobin cause and with whom he would shortly no longer be on speaking terms, Chénier realized that only a thin line separated solemn majesty and dedication to principles of justice from the violence brought about by those who lusted for power.

The tone of this poem characterizes Chénier's position during the Revolution and explains in large part why, even in the light of his increasing anti-Jacobin stance, he was not altogether wrong when he repeatedly asserted that he belonged to no political party. Scarfe has contended that Chénier undoubtedly had a hand in drafting the *Déclaration des Amis de la Constitution ci-devant réunis aux Feuillants* of January 6, 1792, a document which he describes as "a declaration of war not only on the unruly Jacobins but on the royalist *émigrés* as well."[7] If, on the other hand, André Chénier aligned himself with no political party but rather with the principles of moderate, representative, constitutional government, it was inevitable that the Jacobins' excesses would make him increasingly opposed to this political faction. It was axiomatic that during the power struggles that occurred during the first three years of the Revolution and which culminated in the Reign of Terror, those who were not clearly pro-Jacobin were judged by the Jacobin leaders to be anti-Jacobin.

The "Ode" typified Chénier's political stance, his sensing that power was inherently anathema to justice. Indeed, it was the increasing conviction of the truth of this dichotomy that made it impossible for him to capitulate to any of the radical revolutionary leaders. Although such maneuvering might have saved his life, it seems beyond his capacity inasmuch as he never recognized the legality of those who directed the government and were then summarily ousted by more powerful factions. He therefore never felt the need to apologize for his views or to ingratiate himself with the self-styled revolutionary leaders.

Inasmuch as this ode was one of the two poems which Chénier actually wrote with the intent of publishing, there is a certain constraint in the work which can be attributed only in part to its cumbersome structure of twenty-two strophes, each comprising nineteen lines. The influence of antiquity is felt from the outset when the poet apostrophized the muse of poetry. The events which led to the Tennis Court Oath were the result of conditions which were not only conducive to political growth but artistic growth as well. The choice of words here ". . . la liberté mâle/ Des arts est le génie heureux;/ . . . nul talent n'est fils de la faveur royale . . ." (". . . virile liberty is the contented genius of the arts . . . No talent is born of royal favor" ["Le Jeu de Paume," Dimoff, vol. 3, p. 230]), echoed the underlying premise of "La République des Lettres" and the *Essai,* namely that genius can flourish only in an atmosphere of freedom, one in which the artist remained free of external political pressures. An important distinction must be made between Chénier and David in this respect, for although Chénier was celebrating a political event, he did not believe in the inherent inviolability of each act committed in the name of the Revolution, as was so clearly the case with David.

According to Chénier, the destiny of the French people was in the hands of the Revolution:

> O peuple deux fois né! peuple vieux et nouveau!
> Tronc rajeuni par les années!

Phénix sorti vivant des cendres du tombeau!
Et vous aussi, salut, vous, porteurs du flambeau
    Qui nous montra nos destinées!

O people twice born! Young and old people!
    Stock made young again by the years!
Phoenix having emerged living from the ashes of the tomb!
And hail to you too, carriers of the flame
    Who will show us our destinies!
                            ("Le Jeu de Paume," Dimoff, vol. 3, p. 238)

As in his "Avis" Chénier counselled the people not to sacrifice
reason by committing crimes. In fact, the last eight stanzas of the
poem reiterate the fundamental points of the "Avis," namely that
bloody outbursts, those "inhuman feelings," are antithetical to
freedom. Lashing out against the demogogues, the "hangmen-
orators" who have incited the people to commit atrocities, Chénier
called upon the "sovereign people," the vast majority of whom one
must assume distinguishable from the rabble rousers, to fear the
"avid courtisans." He went on to state that those who oppress others
abdicate their own freedom. For if freedom is an inalienable right
which "emanates from the heavens," it must be modified by human
reason and intervention. As he admonished in the first line of the
seventeenth stanza: ". . . Ne croyons pas que tout nous soit permis"
("Let us not believe that everything is permitted us" ["Le Jeu de
Paume," Dimoff, vol. 3, p. 240]). Whereas earlier he had spoken of
the monarchy in decidedly pejorative terms he now described the
French kings as much victims of the "infamous corruptors" as are
the people. Admitting how readily the good intentions of a people
can become perverted, he cited two groups of people who threaten
the harmony by contrary, yet parallel, aims: (1) those who desire to
be both slave and despot through their misuses of freedom and (2)
those who prey upon the natural inhibitions of the weak in order to
make them fearful ("Le Jeu de Paume" Dimoff, vol. 3, p. 241).

Sensing that fanaticism is one of the worst enemies of justice, the
poet spoke out in favor of moderation and good sense, stressing that
it is better to let those guilty of some crime go free than to commit
outrages against the innocent in a fit of overzealous and misguided
patriotism.

In his conclusion Chénier repeated his conviction that justice and
human freedoms, conditions to which all men have the right to
aspire, must be learned. Liberty in fact is inextricably linked to the

law ("Legislating Liberty"). For freedom stands as an eternal value against which human institutions, bound by temporal and spatial considerations, must ultimately be judged. The concluding lines of the ode are an apotheosis of the eternal values of freedom and thereby take the reader far from the specific events of the Tennis Court Oath to the lasting order which can arise only when liberty is seen as the supreme arbiter of historical actions. As the poem concludes, villains, heroes, the wealthy, the poor, the rabble, the politically powerful — all are washed away in a sea of destiny asserting itself:

> La Nécessité traîne, inflexible et puissante,
> A ce tribunal souverain
> Votre majesté chancelante:
> Là seront recueillis les pleurs du genre humain:
> Là, juge incorruptible, et la main sur sa foudre,
> Elle entendra le peuple, et les sceptres d'airain
> Disparaîtront, réduits en poudre.

> Necessity lingers, inflexible and powerful,
> To this sovereign tribunal
> Your tottering majesty:
> There the cries of the human species will be gathered;
> There, incorruptible judge, and the hand on its thunderbolt
> It will hear the people and the bronze scepters
> Will disappear, reduced to powder.
> ("Le Jeu de Paume," Dimoff, vol. 3, pp. 243 - 244)

Emile Faguet's observation may well serve as a summation of this poem: "The 'Ode au Jeu de Paume' is above all the rapid recounting and by great frescos, the pindaric history of the birth of the Assemblée Nationale, but it is then an exterior and interior political program, expressing Chénier's ideas and those of his friends: Sieyès, Condorcet, Bailly, La Fayette."[8]

B. *Andre Chénier and the French Monarchy*

1. *The Summer of 1791:* Le Moniteur

The second phase of André Chénier's involvement with the Revolution can be said to commence with his permanent return to Paris in April, 1791, and end with the execution of Louis XVI on January 21, 1793. This period was marked by a series of letters in *Le*

Moniteur followed by a series of articles for the *Journal de Paris* which were increasingly anti-Jacobin in tone, by the writing of the first *iambe*, the "Hymne aux Suisses de Châteauvieux," and by Chénier's being forced to go into hiding in the summer of 1792, so intense had the revolutionary fervor become.

When he first returned to Paris in June, 1790, Chénier had worked with François de Pange in an unsuccessful effort to revitalize the *Mémoires de la Société de 1789*. During this period he was also in contact with Louis Trudaine and his wife. The person with whom he was most closely associated during the winter of 1790 - 1791 was Louis David. On April 21 a musical gathering of one hundred fifty persons, including Chénier's mistress, Mme de Bonneuil, was disrupted by an unruly crowd who claimed they were breaking up a royalist meeting. The article which resulted from this incident, "Les Autels de la peur" ("The Altars of Fear"), unpublished until 1819, was, as Scarfe points out, a work of such power and modernity that it had the honor of being circulated by the Resistance during World War II.[9] The sarcasm of this article is bolder than any work that preceded it and may be said to constitute an *iambe* in prose. What is distinctly modern in Chénier's essay was his recognition that internal psychological factors rather than external events had enabled the revolutionary movement to triumph over legality. Mob rule had predicated itself on fear. The very term "antipatriot" had been sufficient to cause great waves of emotionalism among the masses while the same word served as an odious pretext for cowardice. Significantly, Chénier refrained from his earlier tactic of lauding the virtue of the French people in an effort to move them in that direction. Here, for the first time, he conceded that "the wicked are united . . . the good have only innocence and do not have the courage of virtue" ("Autels," Pléiade, p. 362). As an indictment of the mounting panic which was eroding the foundations of legally organized government, the "Autels de la peur" marked Chénier's growing disenchantment and suggested that he was now forced to admit that perhaps he had been championing a lost cause.

The summer of 1791 brought a relative hiatus to André Chénier's activity. Louis XVI's attempted flight to Varennes on June 20 sounded the death knell for the already precarious French monarchy. Although not indifferent to the personal fate of the king, Chénier had by now pinned his hopes on the Constitution which was nearly finished, for he felt that the principles of liberty would not be implemented until the machinery to ensure a universal obedience to law was in operation. Through that summer, therefore, Chénier argued for the establishment of constitutional measures which would provide the entire nation with the means of recognizing and upholding the law and for the restitution of discriminatory measures taken during the first years of the Revolution. Despite his disgust with the tactics taken by some émigrés who had fled to London and with the decadence of the clergy, he wished émigrés to be allowed to return to France and for clergy to be treated with equity.

Meanwhile, revolutionary fervor had been growing. On July 17, 1791, there was a demonstration at the Champ-de-Mars by a large crowd who wished to demonstrate their determination to force the king to abdicate. On September 14, the very day that Louis XVI swore to uphold the Constitution which had been read at a session of the assembly on August 5, M. de la Luzerne, Chénier's employer at the London embassy, died. Left without a means of employment, Chénier unsuccessfully attempted to obtain the post of diplomatic representative in Switzerland, a post which went to Barthélemy, his older and more experienced colleague in London. Later, his having sought the Swiss position and written to Barthélemy to have his personal effects sent to Paris, would be used by the Jacobins in their efforts to prove that Chénier, in correspondence with foreign agents, was an enemy of the country. At the same time, the Jacobins would not hesitate to point to Chénier's collaboration with a journal deemed clearly antirevolutionary.

At the beginning of 1792 Chénier was once again working with his old friend François de Pange, this time for the *Journal de Paris*. The articles written for this publication from the beginning of 1792 to the end of the summer show an increasingly open attack on the Jacobins. By this time the Jacobins, who at the writing of the "Avis" in 1790 were mainly working as individuals, had banded together and constituted a network of some eight hundred clubs throughout France.

2.   "Hymne aux Suisses de Châteauvieux"

Chénier reacted vehemently to the proposed celebration by the Jacobins of the amnestied Swiss mercenaries who, in August, 1790, had mutinied against the king's regiments. Those who had not been executed had been sentenced to forced labor. The idea of having these ex-convicts march on the capital in triumph was the work of the Jacobins who saw it as another occasion to attack the king's authority and sway the masses. Chénier's biting satire on the incident has been compared to the highest levels of wit and irony produced by La Fontaine and Voltaire. His very choice of the word "hymne" in his title designates the satirical spirit under which he wished to present the Jacobins' penchant for ceremonial pomp. Moreover, the "Hymne aux Suisses de Châteauvieux" has the distinction of being his first *iambe*.

Traditionally, the *iambe* has been a satiric poem of variable length in *rimes croisées* (abab dcdc, etc.) in which alexandrines alternate throughout with octosyllabics. The satiric sense of the term *iambe* is rooted in a very ancient tradition deriving from the notoriously bitter iambics of the Greek poet Archilochus who lived during the eighth or seventh century B.C. It was Chénier, however, who caused the *iambe* to come into French as a generic term with his posthumously published work. Earlier poets such as Jean-Baptiste Rousseau had written poems resembling *iambes* with the verses disposed in quatrains. Chénier's introducing lines of eight and twelve syllables, an innovation, allowed him to convey the fullest measure of sarcasm by the use of jolting rhythms.

The noble warriors invoked by Chénier in the name of a divine triumph have the honor, he wrote, of having been responsible for spilling the blood of Desilles, massacred by his own soldiers when he attempted to forestall the insurgents from firing on the troops sent against them. Chénier went on to "praise" in lethal invective the mentality that would elevate Jourdan, the leader of the Avignon massacres, and send LaFayette to the scaffold. Addressing himself to the forty murderers celebrated by Robespierre at a gathering of Jacobins and to their defense attorney, Collot-d'Herbois, he suggested that the entire contingent of Jacobins were low murderers when he linked together "la vertu, la taverne, et le secours des piques" ("virtue, the tavern, and the aid of spades" [Dimoff, vol. 3, p. 261]). In his conclusion he spoke of the first argonauts, implying that modern sailors about to capsize take courage from the example of the Swiss of Collot-d'Herbois.

3.   *The Mounting Attack on the Jacobins*

Within a week after the celebration in honor of the Swiss mercenaries on April 15 its full implications on the demoralized French people were seen. On April 20 Louis XVI had declared war on Austria and shortly thereafter the French army crumbled under the first half-hearted attacks it had to face in Belgium.

Still, in his *Journal de Paris* articles Chénier refused to accede to pessimism and intensified his appeal to his countrymen to be wary of so-called patriotic societies which are creating more internal strife than the wars on the continents. He enjoined the French people to forget their differences and show, in their support of their army, that patriotism is not the hatred of all insubordination and liberty is not the freedom to commit any crime, a theme he was to take up again on July 5 when he wrote that if not all Frenchmen can be at the head of an army like LaFayette, they can at least wage their own war against the common enemy. ("De la nécessité de l'union," — "On the Necessity of Union" ["Pléiade, p. 349]). This enemy had already been openly identified in the May 8 article, no longer as members of patriotic societies but as Jacobins ("Le Parti des Jacobins," — "The Party of the Jacobins" [Pléiade, pp. 312 - 315]). Although he refrained from mentioning specific names, his readers could easily identify the Jacobin leaders held up as false prophets.

On June 24 Chénier openly took the defense of the king ("La Journée du 20 Juin," — "The Day of June 20"), threatened four days earlier by a mob of 8,000 persons who stormed the Tuileries. He based his argument on the principle that justice must apply to king and subject alike.

Because of his open attack on the Jacobins and his defense of the king, Chénier found it necessary to leave Paris during the summer of 1792, and he spent most of his time with Fanny Lecoulteux in Louveciennes. Events were moving at a rapid pace toward the downfall of the monarchy. On August 10 the Tuileries were invaded and the royal family was forced to take refuge with the assembly. The arrested king was supposed to defend himself before a Revolutionary Tribunal. In the conclusion of a letter to his father, dated September 22, 1792, Chénier admitted that he had already deluded himself into thinking that the Revolution would follow a moderate course. In fact, one week later there appeared the first sign that Chénier recognized the possibility of incurring personal danger. As events turned out, he was forced to spend the last months of 1792 in hiding in Rouen and Le Havre.

4.   *The Trial and Death of Louis XVI*

André Chénier's role in the document prepared by Malesherbes, the king's chief defense lawyer, has always been the subject of controversy. To the degree, however, that the unspoken notes found among Chénier's manuscripts differ considerably from those of the king's official defender, it is reasonable to assume that he did not play an open role in the defense. Moreover, there is no mention of his having participated in a formal capacity in the trial of Louis XVI in the *acte d'accusation* drawn up against him at Saint Lazare. Five principal points emerge from Chénier's notes:

1) A priori, it was necessary to determine the legality of the Constitution.

2) If this step did not suffice to disrupt the process, then it would be necessary to assure the king of all rights of the defense.

3) Having done this, the defense lawyers should not plead the complete innocence of the king.

4) In the event that the king is judged guilty, his crime should be that he did not know how to govern.

5) Finally, it follows that the condemnation to death of an ignorant man cannot be based on the fallacy that he was destined to be born of royal blood.[10]

With the execution of the king on January 21, 1793, the creation of a Revolutionary Tribunal on March 10, the assassination of Marat by Charlotte Corday on July 13, and mass executions on the guillotine, the period of the Revolution known as the Reign of Terror came into being. Chénier had espoused the principles of legally constituted government and justice for all Frenchmen, regardless of class or occupation. For more than two years he had appealed to love of country and freedom, when in fact self-interest had been the motivating force that internally had created anarchy, a huge network of spies and the shedding of French blood by Frenchmen. Chénier was certainly not always politically astute and his writings suggest, moreover, that at times he was singularly impressed by the sound of his own rhetoric. On the other hand, he did sound with unrelenting dignity a note of moderation in principles of government and morality and reason, one of the last eighteenth century vestiges of the philosophic current that had produced Montesquieu, Voltaire, and Rousseau.

A letter of October 28, 1792, written in response to the German author Wieland and addressed to Brodelet, a lawyer and counselor to the king, less than two months before the king's execution, suggests that Chénier had emerged from his political activism thoroughly disheartened with respect to the prospect of the Revolution's taking a turn in the direction of enlightenment and thereby convinced that further entanglements were futile:

What am I doing in the Revolution? Nothing thanks to Heaven, absolutely nothing. That is what I promised myself from the beginning, knowing already from the beginning that the times of Revolutions are never those of men who are upright and steadfast in their principles, who want neither to lead or follow factions and who loathe all intrigue. Distressed by the evils which I saw and those which I predicted, I have in the course of the Revolution, published, from time to time, reflections which I believed useful, and I haven't changed my opinion. This frankness, which prevented nothing, has been worth only a great deal of hatred, persecutions, and maligning. Therefore I am all the more determined not to take any active part in public affairs and, limiting myself in my solitude, to make some wishes, for the liberty, tranquility and happiness of the Republic, which, to tell the truth, vastly exceed my hopes. . . .

("A M. Brodelet," Pléiade, p. 798)

5. *Fanny, Charlotte Corday, and Versailles*

In the three months following the execution of the king, the Jacobins tightened their hold on France with the creation of the Revolutionary Tribunal and the Committee of Public Safety. When Chénier learned in April that his father had been suspected of being lukewarm in matters of patriotism he made up his mind to leave Paris. In going to Versailles he chose not only the capital of the department represented in the Convention by his brother Marie-Joseph but also a retreat near Louveciennes, the home of Fanny Lecoulteux, whom he had known since 1787. From the spring of 1787 to 1793 Chénier completed a series of six poems dedicated to Fanny, the "Ode à Marie-Anne-Charlotte Corday" and the "Ode à Versailles." These works represent a significant progression in the integration of Chénier's development as a political analyst and poet. If the Fanny cycle revealed the love poet and the "Ode à Marie-Anne-Charlotte Corday" the commemoration of a counter-revolutionary event, the "Ode à Versailles" evoked at once the elusive charm of love as well as the passing of a civilization.

6. *The Fanny Cycle*

The odes Chénier wrote for Fanny Lecoulteux are characterized by their wide variety of verse forms and by the intensity of the emotion evoked by the poet. Despite the rapidity with which events were moving in the capital, the months Chénier spent with Fanny were filled with sentimental walks in the country and by his accompany-

ing her as she performed works of charity for her less fortunate
neighbors in the vicinity of Louveciennes. His first poem to Fanny
had been written in 1790 before he left for London. The image of
Fanny as a mother had inspired him to speak of her maternal bed in
saintly terms. The death of Fanny's daughter two years later, the
current political climate, the deep adoration that Chénier felt for
this woman, and Fanny's tenderness toward her child all contributed
to the vision of ethereal beauty and elusive happiness in these
poems.

In the first ode Fanny is extolled as a symbol of motherhood but a
"mère craintive" ("timid mother"). The images of fecundity —
"Précurseurs de l'automne, ô fruits nés d'une terre . . . des soleils du
midi" ("Precursors of autumn, a harvest . . . midday suns" [Dimoff,
vol. 3, p. 209]) are contrasted with the delicate beauty of Fanny's
daughter, "sa fille aux doux yeux, fleur débile" ("her daughter with
soft eyes, sickly flower" [Dimoff, vol. 3, p. 209]). The vicissitudes of
life, characterized as a "péril funeste" ("morbid siege"), are
countered by the "tendre défiance" ("tender defiance") of Fanny's
maternal love. The *alliance de mots* here evokes a melancholy revery
as the poet contemplates joys that cannot endure. Chénier's
Neoplatonic love for Fanny came to assume the beatific aura of the
one who inspires such love. Imploring the gods to keep suffering and
care far from his beloved's heart, the poet expresses his willingness
to have died in place of her child in order to have spared her the incomparable grief of having endured such a loss.

The tone of the fourth ode, which begins with a resounding
negative, "Non," is much more aggressive than the first. As in the
first ode the full measure of Chénier's love can be expressed only in
death. Although the theme of the desperate lover undergoing the
agonies of unrequited love is common to both the songs of the
medieval troubadours and Preromantic literature, Chénier managed
in these odes to transcend the limits of literary convention and sing
of a chaste and profound love on a note of obscured melancholy.

The most famous of the odes to Fanny, the fifth, was set to music
in the nineteenth century, beginning with the words: "Fanny,
l'heureux mortel qui prés de toi respire" ("Fanny, the happy mortal
who breathes near you" [Dimoff, vol. 3, p. 213]). Once again the
purity of his love cannot be sustained in earthly surroundings and
death alone provides release. What is most original in this ode and
the others in the cycle is that Fanny is at once idealized and envisaged in terms of human flesh and blood. A series of *enjambements* are utilized to describe Fanny's attributes:

> La grâce, la candeurs, la naïve innocence
>   Ont, depuis ton enfance
> De tout ce qui peut plaire enrichi ta beauté.

> Grace, candor, naïve innocence
> Have, since your childhood
> Enriched your beauty with everything that can please.
> (Dimoff, vol. 3, p. 213)

These *enjambements* convey the eternal character of these qualities that time cannot efface. In the second stanza Fanny's spiritual traits are associated with earthly images, yet the inspirational character of Fanny's being remains as discernible as ever: ". . . roses de jeunesse/ Ces roses de pudeur charmes plus séduisants" ("Roses of youth, roses of modesty, more seducing charms" [Dimoff, vol. 3, p. 214]). Such is the hold of Fanny on the poet that he is incapable of speaking to her in everyday circumstances. The dialogues that transpire between the poet and his idolized love belong to the realm of an imagined extraterrestrial, extratemporal locale in which the full measure and purity of Chénier's love would be recognized and hence vindicated. His fervent desire is that he might be able to fix his heart on her in his absence so that she would be as totally absorbed in him as he is in her. Wandering in the forests with her image ever present, he is the fawn who flees her mortal wound, the one who, out of breath, lies down near pure water and awaits death.

The sixth ode describes the poet's more furtive efforts to fix Fanny's elusive charms. The rhythmic pattern of an octosyllabic, three alexandrines, octosyllabic, and alexandrine, evokes a mood of languid signs and suggests despair alternating with a quickened tempo of hope:

> Quelquefois un souffle rapide
> Obscurcit un moment sous sa vapeur humide
> L'or, qui reprend soudain sa brillante couleur.

> Sometimes a rapid breath obscures for a moment
> Under its humid vapor
> The gold, which suddenly resumes its brilliant color.
> (Dimoff, vol. 3, p. 215)

Chénier longs for one moment of her inflamed breath (Fanny has the power to both vivify and kill), of her rosy beauty which has withered the flower by virtue of its incomparable quality. The romantic agony depicted here, associated with the poet's finding a bitter-sweet consolation, is his very suffering. At the conclusion of the poem Fanny becomes indistinguishable from life itself, for her image, recalled in his heart, calms the soul that it has troubled. Love is no longer exclusively Neoplatonic or linked to an intellectual state of being but has become, in a lyric of poignant beauty, ineluctably likened to destiny itself:

> Vivre est te regarder, et t'aimer, te le dire;
>   Et quand tu daignes me sourire,
> Le lit de Vénus même est sans prix à mes yeux.

> To live is to gaze upon you, and love you, and to speak
>   to you about this love,
> And when you deign to smile at me
> The very bed of Venus is priceless to my eyes.
>   (Dimoff, vol. 3, p. 217)

7. "Ode à Marie-Anne-Charlotte Corday"

The "Ode à Marie-Anne-Charlotte Corday" marked an important stage in André Chénier's artistic development, for it shows that, like Voltaire, who found it necessary upon returning from England to explore the possibilities of the *conte philosophique* as a means of providing an appropriate form for the new content of his thought, Chénier had to experiment with a new form to give full expression to his anger when learning the decision of Robespierre and his followers to proclaim a special day of mourning for the assassinated Marat. This poem, labeled an ode, is much more somber than the "Hymne aux Suisses de Châteauvieux," in which Chénier similarly viewed his countrymen's definition of heroism with the greatest skepticism and sarcasm.

As in one of the odes to Fanny, Chénier began this work with an interjection "Quoi!" ("What!") which suggests his utter amazement that groups of men, whether sincere or hypocritical, were going to honor Marat. The particular forthcoming event, the mourning of Marat, which Chénier found odious, is immediately seen within the framework of classical antiquity and takes on the symbolism of a transgression against nature, that is, against the gods:

> Des fanges du Parnasse un impudent reptile
> Vomit un hymne infâme au pied de ses autels.

From the filth of Parnasse an impudent reptile
Vomits an infamous hymn at the foot of his altars.
("Ode à Marie-Anne-Charlotte Corday," Dimoff, vol. 3, p. 252)

The unbroken chain of alexandrines conferred a weighty ponderous tone to Chénier's declamations to the entire French nation whereas the repetition of interjections of commands ("Va, va") created the feeling at the same time that Chénier was engaged in a personal dialogue with one of Marat's admirers.

After portraying the assassination of Marat as the exorcising of a black demon, a pestilence, which was an honor to the gods, Chénier addressed himself once again to his countrymen who, in preparing a feast for the butchered monster Marat, revealed themselves worthy of his fate. Their bloodthirsty ways are contrasted with the manner of a Corday who was willing to face death to uphold her most vaunted principles. Charlotte Corday's act had cosmic repercussions. Cheerful, from all outward appearances, she willed her power to "hit mountains with flashes of lightning and swell the waters of the sea" ([Dimoff, vol. 3, p. 253). Alliteration and a slow, deliberate rhythm conferred a sense of inexorable destiny on the actions of this heroine whom Chénier likened to a goddess of antiquity:

Belle, jeune, brilliante, aux bourreaux amenée,
Tu semblais t'avancer sur le char d'hyménée.

Beautiful, young, brilliant, led to the hangmen,
You seemed to advance on a wedding chariot.
("Ode à Marie-Anne-Charlotte Corday," Dimoff, vol. 3, p. 253)

Virtue, which alone is free, is contrasted with the "immortal shame" of France, a striking *alliance de mots*. Significantly, Chénier did not separate himself from the cowardly emasculated crowd of men in whose midst Corday's "masculine courage" was singular.

In the twelfth stanza Chénier's view of Charlotte Corday's act assumed a new dimension. She was no longer seen as aspiring to lift the yoke of tyranny from her compatriots or as a metaphor of an inspired Greek goddess. She had touched the noblest spirit of the French people: "Non; tu ne pensais pas qu'aux mânes de la France" ("No; you did not think only of the departed spirits of France" [Dimoff, vol. 3, p. 254]) — and in thus becoming the embodiment of mankind's universal quest for freedom, has joined the ranks of an

earlier woman-deliverer of France, Jeanne d'Arc, whom Virtue ap-
plauded when her countrymen demanded her death.

Chénier's "Ode à Marie-Anne-Charlotte Corday" vibrates with
both irony and rage. Seen as a heroic figure from the perspective of
both a contemporary tableau and the deities of ancient mythology,
Charlotte Corday in Chénier's hands ultimately found her place in
history as a solitary, driven, yet no less human, embodiment of virtue in the face of overwhelming evil.

8. "Ode à Versailles"

Chénier's "Ode à Versailles," written most likely in the fall of
1793, has been called by Sainte-Beuve "the most beautiful, the most
complete of André Chénier's works, a royal elegy in all its glory."[11]
Utilizing a structural device in which both alexandrines and octosyllabics appear in each of the ten strophes, Chénier began the ode by
evoking the majesty of Versailles, a city of "marbres vivants,
berceaux antiques,/ Par les Dieux et les rois Elysée embelli" ("living
marbles, ancient cradle,/ An Elysium embellished by the Gods and
kings" [Dimoff, vol. 3, p. 218]). Yet the majesty of a forsaken palace
did not lead the poet to sterile, lifeless thoughts of death, for the
memory of a livelier, inhabited court delivered him from blighting
memories just as dew relieves a plant in draught. Trees and forests
console the poet who has sought tranquillity and obliteration of
painful events in a secluded house overlooking the avenues of elms
and the countryside where he walks. For Versailles, sheltered though
it may be, also evoked for Chénier a passing civilization whence all
has fled — royal chariots, pomp, and "des gardes les nocturnes
veilles" ("thy marching night watch on alert" [Dimoff, vol. 3,
p. 218)]. Versailles, no longer the scene of royal grandeur, is now inhabited only by the gods of solitude, repose, and the arts.

Yet, life is not beyond repair because with each breath that he
takes a woman haunts his thoughts and her presence enables him to
bear the weight of life. Nowhere perhaps is the versatility of Chénier's expression as a love poet more apparent, for the same Fanny,
who had in the earlier odes inspired him with the idea of committing
the ultimate act of self-sacrifice, now provided the sole reason for
clinging to life. Love is an elixir: "J'aime; je vis. Heureux rivage!"
("I love; I live. Immortal bank" [Dimoff, vol. 3, p. 219]). His
beloved has restored to him his poetic fertility; it is in the shady
groves, where he meditated on her, that his lines took shape: "Pour

elle seule encore abonde/ Cette source, jadis féconde" ("For her alone comes forth again/ This source once ripe" [Dimoff, vol. 3, p. 219]).

Yet Versailles evoked not only sun-drenched days filled with countryside walks and thoughts of Fanny but also the reign of lawlessness and crimes. Versailles could be the scene of youth and love only when justice prevailed over France. At the present time, however, Versailles' rolling hills and cooling retreats brought to mind mourning and a procession of persons destined to die by the ruling barbarians.

Scarfe's characterization of the ode as fugal has much merit inasmuch as the various themes do in fact interweave here without dissonance.[12] Written at the height of the Reign of Terror when Chénier's own safety and that of Fanny were under constant threat, the ode is held together by the poet's subtle orchestration of contrasting themes: the yearning for a legally reconstituted society as opposed to the bygone splendor of Versailles, symbol of excess yet not affording a brief respite from the bloodsoaked capital; an evocation of the power of the passions, yet an awareness that the need for reason in matters of state could not be ignored. In this work the troubadour as love poet and as voice of the Revolution became as one.

III   *The Last Phase*

Since the end of April, 1793, Chénier had been living the clandestine life of an alleged suspect in Versailles. In March of that year the Revolutionary Tribunal, in conjunction with the Committee for Public Safety, had accelerated its work of spying and informing and the guillotine was working overtime. After the assassination of Marat in July revolutionary fervor increased even more. In September a *Loi des suspects*, which did away with the last semblance of law, was passed and was responsible for the carnage known as the September Massacres. For more than a year the *Declaration of the Rights of Man* and most of the Constitution had been quietly buried. By December of that year the entire Lecoulteux family was imprisoned. On March 7, 1794, on one of his periodic trips to Paris, Chénier was arrested at Passy while visiting the Marquis de Pastoret for whose arrest a warrant had been taken out only three days earlier. The exact nature of his visit is not known. Loggins states that Chénier may have wished to deliver a message to the

Pastorets from François de Pange, whereas Scarfe contends that de Pange had accompanied Chénier to Passy but managed to escape.[13] When interrogated, Chénier was asked routine questions about his identity and living quarters. The matter of his having received letters from "enemies of the Republic" and from England in particular was dwelt on at greater length. Chénier's response concerning Barthélemy's letter about his personal effects did not satisfy his interrogators who proceeded to launch a new series of questions. Other points of contention were Chénier's not having borne arms against the king on August 10, 1792, his friendship with the aristocratic Trudaines, his suspicious intent of going to Versailles late at night, and his less than deferential manner when questioned by a Revolutionary Tribunal.

On the following day Chénier was taken to the Luxembourg. For reasons unknown he was not admitted there and was subsequently taken to the prison of Saint-Lazare. The poet Roucher was also interned, as was Aimée de Coigny, duchesse de Fleury, the subject of what is perhaps Chénier's most famous work, "La Jeune Captive." On the same day a formal warrant was sent to Saint-Lazare from Passy. It is generally agreed that Louis Chénier's intervention on his son's behalf was more harmful than beneficial inasmuch as he called attention to his son's diatribes against the Jacobins when he cited the articles of *Le Moniteur* and the *Journal de Paris*.

At the end of May the government directed its attention to what was called the "conspiration des prisons" ("conspiracy of prisons"). On June 21 Robespierre and the Committee of Public Safety instituted the necessary machinery to investigate these plots. While conditions in Saint-Lazare became increasingly worse, Chénier was writing his *iambes* on brown laundry paper. By April visits of relatives in the courtyard had been proscribed. On July 24 the poets André Chénier and Roucher were formally charged together by Fouquier of being enemies of the people by virtue of their counter-revolutionary activities.

The charges that could be proved, that they were defenders of the principles of the Constitution, had attacked the Jacobins, and had written for the *Journal de Paris*, were not legal offenses. Moreover, Chénier was confused in a further list of charges with his brother Louis-Sauveur. How Chénier handled the matter has never been clear but his family loyalty seems to have excluded the possibility that he would have cleared himself of some charges arising from mistaken identity by calling attention to his brother.

During the actual trial on July 25 Chénier was attacked for his having condemned the march on the Tuilleries, his failure to participate in the overthrow of the monarchy, and his attack on the Swiss of Châteauvieux. Having been judged guilty by the jury's verdict, André Chénier was guillotined that same afternoon on what is known as the Place de la Nation.

It is not my intention to weigh in great detail the morality of Chénier's arrest, conviction, and execution, for to do so would be to enter into a lengthy discussion of the various factions, personalities, and internal and external events that occurred during the revolutionary years. Obviously, reactions to the circumstances of Chénier's death are colored by the degree to which one believes in the wisdom of the Revolution. The problem is complicated by the fact that changes affecting the everyday life of millions of persons occurred extremely rapidly during the years from 1789 to the end of the century, and so the great instability of conditions during this period necessitates the interpretation of events against the larger background of general conditions in France and the situation in other countries.

The French Revolution and André Chénier's role, in particular, have generally elicited extreme responses. Thus, Walter, the editor of the Pléiade edition of Chénier's works, having taken a Marxist stand toward the Revolution, concluded that Chénier was its avowed enemy. In a full-length study of Chénier, Walter contended nonetheless that Chénier was sincere in his actions:

He believed and very sincerely that during a time of Revolution, severe and honest censors are needed who, removed from all partisan thought, devote themselves to condemning all the injustices and excesses without distinguishing those who are responsible for them. He did not understand . . . that impartiality was the cloak behind which more and more the most dedicated royalists hid themselves.[14]

Yet, in the introduction to the same work Walter noted that Chénier's poems were unknown to all but a handful of persons and suggested that the Revolution was somehow justified in removing from its midst an implacable enemy:

It isn't the tender elegic, the soft Theocritus whom the latter [the men of the Revolution] sent to the guillotine, but an unyielding enemy who had announced decisively that he saw only one way out of the struggle: their extermination or his. I say then and I repeat it: it is a dangerous political adversary whom the revolutionaries of the year II killed at the scaffold. . . .[15]

More typically, however, Chénier has been viewed as a martyr to freedom: ". . . his gallant struggle against overwhelming odds will always shed lustre on him while his sacrifice of himself for principle, and his tragic death, must always lend a peculiar interest to his literary achievement."[16]

It is reasonable to conclude that if André Chénier attacked many inequities of the Ancien Régime and praised the idealism which seemed to characterize the opening moments of the Revolution, he came to view with greater alarm what he considered the lawlessness, mob rule, excessive emotionalism, and power struggles of the nation in general and the Jacobins in particular. Perhaps a fitting commentary on Chénier's relationship to the Revolution, before turning to discuss the poems he wrote in the last months of his life, is Chénier's own words in an incomplete play, *Les Initiés*, sketched during the time he was writing the odes to Charlotte Corday and to Versailles. Writing of himself in the third person Chénier planned to conclude his preface with these words:

He is weary of sharing the shame of the many, many Frenchmen who in secret abhor as does he and at the same time by their silence encourage gangs of malefactors who are daily committing unspeakably base crimes. When the most vulgar of burlesque stages, clamoring taverns and houses of debauchery vomit up thousands of legislators, magistrates and generals who rise from this debris to act, as they claim, on behalf of the motherland, he, this one, has another end in sight. And he believes that his country will say of him at a future time: "This country, which at that horrendous epoch produced so many champions of stupidity and baseness, produced at the same time men who renounced neither their reason nor their conscience. Though they witnessed the triumph of Vice, they remained in touch with Virtue and were not ashamed to be known as men of good will. In those times of violence they had the courage to speak of justice; in those times of mad impulsiveness they continued to weigh and reflect; in those times of blatant hypocrisy they did not pretend to be base in order not to be troubled by the slaughter of the innocent. Nor did they hide their aversion for butchers who knew no limits to their crimes in order to heap rewards on themselves and their kind and, at the same time, punish their opponents. And a man named A. C. was one of at least five or six who refused to bow to crowded assassins or shake with hands tainted by murder or dine with those who had drunk the blood of their countrymen." (Pléiade, p. 581)

It is senseless to argue to what degree André Chénier favored the French Revolution since his writings from 1790 to 1794 indicate very clearly that he envisaged reform within the existing order and opposed with increasing fervor the anarchy which had spread throughout France. Liberal in his attitudes towards the abolishment of privilege and civil equality for all citizens before the law, he was essentially conservative, as Montesquieu and Voltaire had been before him, in his belief that constitutional separation of powers along English models provided the best safeguards against tyranny. Mornet, conceding that eighteenth century philosophy transformed men's minds by making them lose their habit of respect for tradition, concluded nonetheless that "not one of the philosophers would be considered a revolutionist, and they all profoundly distrusted popular government and even liberty."[17]

In our own times Albert Camus has posited his hopes on rebellion, a concept based on the Greek ideal of measure, a denial that all is permitted in the name of an ideal or an unfolding historical process and a fundamental affirmation of the value of life as opposed to Jean-Paul Sartre's brand of revolution in which the ends justify the means. André Chénier, an earlier assimilator of Greek thought, was an indisputable forerunner of Camus in this debate.

In his keynote address to the Fourth International Enlightenment Congress held at Yale University in July, 1975, Peter Gay characterized the basic tenets of eighteenth century French thought in terms of a growing conviction among Frenchmen that the nobles were parasites, the bourgeoisie were the greatest contributors to the welfare of the country, and the lower classes were to be feared. André Chénier's writings show that he believed in the truth of this distinction in part but only in part and never rigidly or fanatically. From his perspective as a moralist he spoke of principles that transcended social class or party lines which, after the outbreak of the Revolution, alienated him from the elements in power. As the Revolution progressed he recognized that the law had become the handmaiden of anarchy and died in large part because he steadfastly held to this view.

CHAPTER 6

The Last Poems

ACCORDING to Scarfe it was probably in the fall of 1793 that Chénier returned to the *iambe* form which he had used the previous year in the "Hymne aux Suisses de Châteauvieux."[1] These *iambes* and mostly the odes written during Chénier's last year convey all the vibrations of a man thoroughly revolted and shuddering with indignation before the sight of mass executions. Although Chénier's prose writings from 1790 to 1792 are a rich source of information about his views on law, government, and, above all, human nature, the last poems represent the most intensely personal artistic record of every phase of Chénier's existence: French citizen, Everyman confronting death, the sensitive human being moved by the fate of a beautiful young woman about to die, ill-treated brother, and poet communicating to future generations his faith in freedom. If it is true that Louis David's paintings represent the highest form of official revolutionary art, it is also true that Chénier's last poems, the spontaneous reaction of the artist's inner life to the external events of the Revolution, recall in lyrical satire the invectives of the Old Testament prophets.

With the Revolution's growing encroachment on Chénier's safety, the striking rhythms of the alternating alexandrines and octosyllabics of his *iambes* reveal a lessening of any distinction between himself and the French people until ultimately his destiny became thoroughly identifiable in his own mind with that of all humanity. The originality of the *iambes* lies precisely in the fact that they reveal the reactions of one single poet to specific historical events while suggesting the voice of Everyman of all times and of all places, striving to be heard by future generations in less cataclysmic moments of human history.

I *"Marat au Panthéon"*

In November, 1793, Chénier wrote an *iambe* on the occasion of the Convention's intention to remove Marat's body to the Pantheon. The dramatic effect in this poem was achieved by Chénier's juxtaposing the sublime with the base, thus sustaining an unremitting level of sarcasm against those who would stain the majestic arches of the Pantheon with the remains of a public executioner. By the time Chénier wrote this poem, relations with the painter David had come to the point where the same artist who had frequented Chénier's mother's salon and had inspired Chénier by his enormous tableau depicting the Tennis Court Oath could now be the subject of Chénier's bitter irony:

> Pourquoi vois-je David qui larmoie, et prépare
> Sa pallette qui fait des Dieux?

> Why do I see David, who is shedding tears and prepares
> His pallet that makes Gods?
> ("Marat au Panthéon," Dimoff, vol. 3, p. 263)

The fifth line is not only a bombastic outcry: "O ciel! faut-il le croire! ô destins! ô fortune!" ("Oh heavens! must one believe it! oh destiny! oh fortune!" [Dimoff, vol. 3, p. 263]), but suggests also that Chénier viewed contemporary events as crimes against nature. A series of three *enjambements* enabled Chénier to underscore his attack on Barère who had waged an arduous battle to purify the French language of any aristocratic influences. Then, to intensify his attack, Chénier cited an allegedly irrefutable source, Brissot, as proof of the impure vapors that had been exuded everywhere in France. The two *enjambements* in succession created a vivid impression of a heavy cloud, hovering and menacing the French people:

> Brissot, qui n'a jamais menti,
> Dit avoir vu dans l'air d'exhalaisons impures
> Un noir nuage tournoyer,
> Du sang, et de la fange, et toutes les ordures
> Dont se forme un épais bourbier . . .

> Brissot, who has never lied,
> Says that he has seen impure exhalations in the air
> Swirl a black cloud.

Of blood, and of mud, and all the excrement
Of which a thick mire is formed.

("Marat au Panthéon," Dimoff, vol. 3, p. 264)

II "Les Noyades de Nantes"

This *iambe* was written in February or March, 1794, in response to
the arch-Jacobin Carrier's decision to undertake the pacification of
Nantes by drowning 6,000 men, women, and children in the Loire in
December, 1793, and January, 1794. This work is distinguished not
only by its prevailing tone of horror and sharpness of language but
also by its never-ending flow of short staccato phrases that suggest
the jerky movement of waves. Moreover, Chénier's ability to achieve
a plastic quality in his art by depicting details in the manner of a
sculptor is highly evident here and evokes a quality of the bucolics,
in particular the drowning of the young Tarentine.

The cosmic significance of the drownings is immediately conveyed by the suggestion that the forces of nature knew no limits during this carnage:

> Ont-elles par milliers dans les gouffres de Loire
> Vomi des captifs enchaînés?

> Have they by the thousands in the abysses of the Loire
> Vomited the chained captives?

(Dimoff, vol. 3, p. 271)

This image of instant death is contrasted in supreme dramatic irony
with the reaction of its perpetrator, Carrier, to the event: "des cap-
tifs . . . pour son passe-temps amenés" ("the captives . . . led there
for his amusement" [Dimoff, vol. 3, p. 271]).

Having depicted in graphic terms the hordes of innocent people
being swallowed up in a spectacle of ghastly horror which points to
the whitish-grey tones of Delacroix's "Dante and Virgil in Hell,"
Chénier then offered a contrasting tableau, equally emotionally
charged, of the debauched Jacobin leaders responsible for the
holocaust. The Bordeaux wines, claret in color, which Carrier and his
henchmen have drunk to excess, are linked symbolically with the
blood of their victims. By a brilliant stroke Chénier communicated
the kaleidoscopic movement of a society where men exist without
principles. For there is a common element uniting the victims of the
drowning with the women who, jumping to the beds of the
revolutionary leaders, are destined to fall from favor tomorrow and

thereby supplant today's victims. This is a hell where expiation is beyond attainment, where remorse is unknown, where the one responsible for the drownings "mange, boit, rote du sang" ("eats, drinks, and belches blood" [Dimoff, vol. 3, p. 272]). In conclusion, Chénier stated that he viewed his graphically violent and impure language as entirely consonant with the baseness of his subject.

III *"La Jeune Captive"*

Chénier's most famous work, "La Jeune Captive" was inspired by Aimée de Coigny, duchesse de Fleury, whom Chénier met while interned in Saint-Lazare. Separated in 1793 from the duc de Fleury, Aimée de Coigny was destined to escape the scaffold and outlive Chénier by twenty-six years. Twenty-four years old in 1794, she was for Chénier the embodiment of youthful femininity, vigorous and voluptuous. Although it was assumed in the first decades following Chénier's death that he was in love with Aimée, the work of Alfred de Vigny, a distant cousin of this woman, and others, has refuted the thesis that there existed a profound emotion between the two prisoners. Today it is generally conceded that Chénier invested her rather with the attributes of the eternally feminine. The fact that Giordano's opera depicted the couple in mawkishly sentimental terms or that generations of French schoolchildren have had to commit Chénier's words to memory should not obscure the hauntingly lyrical and poignant quality of this ode.

The first seven stanzas comprise the young prisoner's words, overheard by the poet, as she contemplated her imminent death. Her days on earth, likened to the tumescence and evanescence of nature, have not come full circle and only hint in embryonic form at future potential. The realization that the pastoral images of un-plowed wheat and unpicked grapes are linked to a brutal reality is conveyed by the abrupt termination of these images and the words, "Je ne veux pas mourir encore" ("I do not yet wish to die" [Dimoff, vol. 3, p. 222]).

A movement of expansion, suggesting that the prisoner's illusions are still harbored within her breast, quickly gave way to one of self-containment in which the subject's horizons appeared to stretch no further than the prison walls: "Est-ce à moi de mourir?" ("Is it my time to die?" [Dimoff, vol. 3, p. 223]). Sustained by memories, she managed, by not giving in to sentimental bathos, to transmit her determination to the neighboring prisoners.

In the fifth and sixth stanzas images of nature's perpetual cyclical processes are resumed. Life is a journey during which the voyager sees row upon row of elms, paired along the road. The metaphor of the purple grape in the first stanza is now extended to embrace an image of the feasts that life has promised and whose cup the beautiful prisoner's lips have only begun to touch. As a bud that has not yet unfurled into a flower she has had time to feel only "les feux du matin" ("the morning's warmth").

Her last laments contain an impassioned angry diatribe against death and belie her efforts to withstand total despair, she who had dreamed of a life given to love and the arts. Her last words "Je ne veux point mourir encore" ("I do not wish to die yet" [Dimoff, vol. 3, p. 223]) convey at once the reality and the horror of her situation.

Death is lamentable but life is portrayed as not merely sweet, beautiful, and hopeful but also as bitter and troubling. The image of life as a journey had already found its way into eighteenth century French literature and was to become a cliché in nineteenth century Romantic poetry. In its subtle orchestration of themes most common to lyric poetry — the brevity of life, the passing of youth, the inevitability of death — Chénier's "Jeune Captive" stands as one of the most striking examples of lyricism in French poetry, in which controlled sensibility heightened the sense of poignancy and thereby placed Chénier in a tradition that goes back to François Villon, while announcing the work of Victor Hugo and Paul Eluard. Expressing his own fears about the guillotine, Chénier provided an image of men condemned to die, which was no longer associated with rows of prisoners in chains as it had been for Pascal, but rather with an affirmation of life.

IV *"La Fête de L'Être Suprême"*

On May 8, 1794, it was proposed by Robespierre that the recognition by the Revolution of the God of Reason be the occasion for a great festival on June 9. Chénier's poem was written sometime in May before the actual celebration occurred. The prose sketch of the work contained a passage in which Chénier chided the deity for allowing the Jacobins to pay him homage. As is the case in so many of the *iambes* Chénier began with a declamatory statement which, reminiscent of the first lines of a Corneillean drama, gives the impression that the reader has interrupted a dialogue. By refraining from formally identifying his subject, Chénier made the Jacobins all the more fearsome, for to name them would be superfluous, so ignominious have they become. "Ils vivent cependant et de tant de victimes/ les cris ne montent point vers toi" ("They live, however, and from so many victims/ The cries do not reach you" [Dimoff, vol. 3, p. 270]). The contrast between the Old Testament Lord of Hosts to whom Chénier addressed himself here ("ô grand Dieu des armées" — "oh great God of the armies" [Dimoff, vol. 3, p. 270]) and Chénier himself, "un pauvre poète" ("a poor poet"), added a measure of irony and grandeur to Chénier's invective. Imploring God to aid him in his chastisement of the hypocritical Jacobins who make a mockery of the deity by claiming to have a hold on him, he asked to have a pen as mighty as that granted to the originator of the *iambe*, Archilocus, whose instrument was carved from the marble of Paros. Chénier's sense of mission is revealed by jarring rhythms: "Je les vois, j'accours, je les tiens" ("I see them, I run to them, I seize them"). Imprisoned, Chénier has taken up his pen so that future generations and all nature might rail against the perversions of monsters, dastardly knaves who get drunk on human blood and who refrain from butchering men but immolate women. In a striking juxtaposition Chénier reminds his readers to what extent the law itself has become the handmaiden of tyranny: "Ces juges, ces jurés qui frappent l'innocence,/ Hécatombe à leurs tribunaux" ("These judges, these juries who strike innocence,/ Great carnage at their tribunals" [Dimoff, vol. 3, p. 271]).

V   *"Ode à son frère"*

The ode which André Chénier addressed to his brother, written either shortly before his imprisonment or during his stay at Saint-Lazare, reflected the extent to which the Revolution had severely tested the poet's feelings toward his younger brother. In a letter from his father written at the end of 1789, André learned that Marie-Joseph and his mother had thrown their support to the Jacobin factions that would later assume power. The articles in the *Moniteur* and *Journal de Paris* as well as the poem on the Swiss of Châteauvieux, had been a source of bitter friction between the brothers. There is no greater measure of the degree to which the Revolution had divided the two brothers than in the case of the monarchy. Whereas André believed that Louis XVI should be judged according to the same standards of justice as a commoner, a central point in his notes dealing with the trial of the king, Marie-Joseph voted for the death penalty.

The laudatory opening lines of the ode, in which Chénier expressed his wish that his brother might enjoy prosperity, artistic recognition, and a long life, evoke a tone of restraint inasmuch as the poet addressed his brother in the third person. The reverberating "his", "him", and "he" of the first two stanzas, having replaced "your" and "you," convey at once a distance between the poet and his subject which excluded the familiar mode of discourse and the conflicting emotions of concern and disgust.

By the third stanza the bitter sarcasm which prevailed until the end of the ode was unleashed. As in the case of Chénier's writing on the Châteauvieux Swiss there is an immediate tension between the "virtue" which Chénier ascribed to his subject and his knowledge, communicated by the abrupt introduction of the single word "but" at the beginning of the third stanza, that his brother is far from being the defender of virtue against vice. A striking aspect of this ode is the linking of the abstract with the concrete and normally disparate elements (alliance de mots), thus enabling Chénier to give a heightened significance to his portrait of society in danger of destroying itself: "honnêtes douleurs . . . ceux que livre à la hache un fèroce caprice . . . le sceptre du vice,/ Ses caresses, ses dons . . . un généreux courroux" ("honest sufferings" . . . "hatchet-ferocious caprice" . . . the "caresses and gifts of Vice" . . . "a generous anger" [Dimoff, vol. 3, pp. 244 - 245]). The depiction of crime in the last stanza as a "bloodstained idol" is a powerful image that evoked the actions of a nation that has evolved to the point of knowing no legality beyond that of a drawn sword. This ode, recalling earlier iambes in its tone, derived its force from conflicting passions, Chénier's need to vent his anger at his brother's having capitulated to mob rule and his inability to forget that one of the despised Jacobins was his brother. The outward praise rendered the inner scorn more striking and conveyed the conflicting passions of disbelief, anger, family loyalty and, above all, impatience. Finally, the poem is supremely ironic in view of the fact that Chénier was to meet the end that in the first few stanzas of this poem he fervently wished his brother to avoid.

VI   "Saint-Lazare"

The iambe entitled "Saint-Lazare" is not merely a tableau of prison life but, more significantly, is a revealing account of Chénier's attitude toward human nature. It therefore, characteristically of the iambes, expresses conflicting emotions. It is obvious in this poem that a particular event in Chénier's life, his incarceration in Saint-Lazare, enabled him to draw universally applicable conclusions concerning human behavior. What first appears to be a testimony of mankind's capacity to affirm life by continuing to perform mundane tasks in prison — "On vit; on vit infâme . . . il fallut l'être;/ L'infâme après tout mange et dort . . ." ("We live; we live in infamy . . . we must;/ The infamous one after all eats and sleeps . . ." [Dimoff, vol. 3, p. 275]) — becomes an attack on man's inability to face reality. Death has transformed the prisoners from noble creatures to grazing cattle, oblivious to any higher form of thought. By using a series of words which have double meanings ("parcs": parks or enclosures; "poulets": chickens or loveletters), Chénier was able to develop an extended metaphor of the prisoners as animals who were oblivious to the hatchet that awaited them. Their words, no more meaningful than those of the judges who have condemned them to Saint-Lazare, are likened to balloons inflated with wind. The incessant drinking, laughing, and political debating among the prisoners and the seven hundred members of the Convention stops only with the creaking of the hinged door, which announced the selection of the day's victims.

The image provided by the prisoner André Chénier, that of bovine-like men who prattle and dance before an inevitable death to which they seem oblivious, appears to be diametrically opposed to Pascal's image of chained prisoners, but it is in reality made of the same substance. The joyful bound of the prisoners who realize that their time has not yet come is grotesque, a reminder that identification with one's fellow man was, for Chénier, tempered by both vapidity and selfishness. Chénier's psychological insight here is twentieth century in its modernity, for its points at once to Bruno Bettelheim who described in detail the reactions of his fellow prisoners to the Nazi death camps and to George Orwell's statements in *Animal Farm* concerning the ease with which victims can become hangmen.

VII   *"A Ses Amis"*

The *iambe* which Chénier addressed to his friends is compelling because its pastoral images — herdsmen, dogs, and sheep — far from evoking tableaux of rustic tranquility, describe a world in which every creature is a potential predator in his bid for survival. This aspect of human behavior was heightened by Chénier's use of understatement. The first reaction among the friends of the bleating sheep who is about to be slaughtered is one of indifference. Comparing himself to the sheep in the slaughterhouse — "J'ai le même destin" ("I have the same destiny" [Dimoff, vol. 3, p. 273]) — Chénier, too, felt forgotten by the outside world.

In one sense, however, he was not alone, for thousands more will follow him in order to provide a feast for the bloody hooks of the ruling people-king. Chénier's answer to an allegedly rhetorical question, "Que pouvaient mes amis?" ("What could my friends do?"),

> "Oui, de leur main chérie
> Un mot à travers ces barreaux
> Eût versé quelque baume en mon âme flétrie;
> De l'or peut-être à mes bourreaux . . ."

> "Yes, from their cherished hand
> One word across these bars
> Might have soothed my blighted soul;
> Some gold perhaps to my hangmen . . ."
> (Dimoff, vol. 3, p. 273)

allowed him a brief moment of sarcasm and bitterness. Abandoning his death-infested world he turned to the outside and, while enjoining his friends to live, reminded them of their own mortality: "Soyez lents à me suivre" ("Be slow to follow me" [Dimoff, vol. 3, p. 272). The concluding lines, "Vivez, amis; vivez en paix" ("Live, friends, live in peace" [Dimoff, vol. 3, p. 273]), are conciliatory precisely because Chénier sensed that self-interest was innate: "J'ai moi-même, à l'aspect des pleurs de l'infort [une] [sic] Détourné mes regards distraits" ("I, too, have turned my back on the tears of an unfortunate man" [Dimoff, vol. 3, p. 273]). The haunting quality of this poem is the result of Chénier's movement from the particular to the universal and from the opposition of hope with resignation and bitterness with the release found in his newly acquired insight.

Chénier's witnessing the progressively violent turn of the Revolution led him quite naturally to reflect on self-interest and its consequences. Here and elsewhere during the last months of his life he revitalized a tradition that counted La Rochefoucauld and Vauvenargues among its members.

VIII "Comme un dernier rayon"

Chénier's last *iambe*, thought for many years to have been written on the night before his execution, could not have been, as Scarfe has pointed out, inasmuch as Chénier spent that night at the *conciergerie* awaiting trial.[2] It is reasonable to assume, however, that it was written only a few days before his death.

The slow, steady rhythm, creating a sense of inexorability, was a function of Chénier's repeated use of *enjambement,* lines that flow into one another without punctuation. It is death of course that is imminent here and is rendered all the more awesome because the vocabulary of blood-stained altars and infamous assassinations that appeared in the earlier *iambes* has been replaced by that of nature, man's comforter, "un dernier rayon, un dernier zéphy[re]" [sic] ("a last ray of light, a last balmy breeze" [Dimoff, vol. 3, p. 276]). The scaffold is not frequented by ghostly spectres but rather provides the poet one last opportunity to play his lyre. Death is seen as the culmination of a journey, and the poet, in his soporific state, already imagines himself dead: "Le sommeil du tombeau pressera ma paupière./ Avant que de ces deux moitiés/ Ce vers que je commence ait atteint la dernière . . ." ("the sleep of the coffin will press my eyelid/ Before I end this verse which I now chant . . ." [Dimoff, vol. 3, p. 276]).

The rhythm of the poem changed dramatically at line twenty-five when Chénier accentuated the natural pause of the alexandrine ("Eh bien! j'ai trop vécu. Quelle franchise auguste" — "Indeed, I have lived too long. What somber frankness" [Dimoff, vol. 3, p. 277]). At line thirty-five death is suddenly implored:

> Ah! lâches que nous sommes
> Tous, oui tous. Adieu, terre, adieu.
> Vienne, vienne la mort! — Que la mort me délivre!

> Ah! cowardly that we are
> All, yes all. Farewell earth, farewell.
> Come, come death! — May death deliver me!
>
> (Dimoff, vol. 3, p. 277)

Yet his pride enabled him to overcome this weakness. If it is decreed that he will never again take to battle, sword in hand, he will at least be able to serve humanity with another weapon drenched not with blood but with ink.

Although Chénier never abandoned his penchant for the classical precept of measure, the inspiration of this poem is overwhelmingly emotional rather than intellectual. Justice and Truth, apostrophized, are the only gods to whom Chénier can direct his supplication. Begging forgiveness of these deities if he has ever besmirched them, he appealed to them to prolong his life so that he would not die without having exhausted his invective against tyranny. For his pen can "pierce" and "crush" the "bourreaux barbouilleurs de lois" ("hangmen befoulers of laws") in no less mighty a fashion than a swordsman. His writing alone sustains him "O ma plume! fiel, bile, horreur, Dieux de ma vie!/ Par vous seuls je respire encor" ("O my pen! Gall, bile, horror! Gods of my life./ By you alone I still breathe" [Dimoff, vol. 3, p. 278]), and his words, having become synonymous with life itself, outweigh all other considerations: "Je souffre; mais je vis." ("I suffer, but I live" [Dimoff, vol. 3, p. 278]).

His time is limited, however, just as piling additional wax on a dying candle can revive it only temporarily. Seeing his friends persecuted and honest men ruined and put to death the temptation to suicide would have been insurmountable. This mood of self-pity, however, was immediately checked as Chénier affirmed in the last lines his commitment to serve justice and truth by witnessing, until his last breath, the outrages committed against these principles. The image of the day drawing to a close with which the poem began is now resumed, but the end of the journey which began with balmy breezes and strains of the lyre has given way to a descent into the darkest hell. Only by living can Chénier strike a blow against tyranny. His heart, "gros de haine, affamé de justice" ("swollen with hatred, starved for justice" [Dimoff, vol. 3, p. 279]), has become the apotheosis of defiance: "Vertu, pleure si je meurs" ("Virtue, weep if I die" [Dimoff, vol. 3, p. 279]).

Conclusion

A NDRÉ Chénier's work exemplifies the supreme relationship of the artist with his times. As a product of the Enlightenment Chénier absorbed his century's concern with identifying and preserving the forces that had given rise to great civilizations. Like Voltaire and Montesquieu, he explored the relationship between art and society and, while aware of temporal and geographical influences on human institutions, he posited his art on the belief that men throughout history could be more readily defined by their similarities than by their differences. It was this sense of the universal, the depiction of the essence of man's unchanging primary instincts, that he sought to imitate in the works of the ancients.

Throughout his writings Chénier remained consistently flexible in matters of literary doctrine. Believing that poetry must suggest more than it explicitly states, he created in his bucolics a world inhabited by mythological creatures who reveal subtle nuances of man's primary passions. These pieces, miniature tone poems, suggest the merging of Watteau and Fragonard with the colors of antiquity.

Although Chénier was in many ways an eighteenth century man, he remained singularly at odds with the expository mode of the Enlightenment as embodied in the publication of the *Encyclopédie* and in the salon mentality. His elevation of the artist's independence to the status of a literary credo was entirely consonant with his belief that the poet should depict only what he has personally experienced and that he alone is fit to judge his art. His numerous epistles and elegies reflect his feelings on love and friendship and contain themes that foreshadow major concerns of the Romantics, including unrequited love, the passing of time and the impermanence of all human endeavors, yet the sense of alienation that pervades this work is internal rather than material. Because he believed that the artist should be a moral legislator rather than a seer or visionary, he did not find it necessary to transform the world of everyday events into a symbolic vision of reality but looked increasingly within his own experiences to discover his ties with Everyman.

Chénier revived in French poetry a lyrical strain that had been dormant for many generations and which in his century Jean-Jacques Rousseau alone had preserved to such a degree in his prose works. His resuscitation of the self and his unfailing sense of aesthetic taste, his ability to create a wide spectrum of tonal colors through understated use of language, brought his work to the attention of the Romantics and the Parnassians alike. If he took liberties with the hallowed alexandrine, he did so without ceremony, and his poetics, embracing Boileau's adherence to order and natural expression, did not deal with technical matters but stressed, in the manner of the Greeks, the primacy of the passions and the need to achieve an integration of life and art.

While revitalizing poetry, André Chénier exhibited few of the nineteenth century's penchants for systems. It is in vain that one searches in his work for Lamartine's sense of communion with nature, for Victor Hugo's cosmic vision, for Balzac's scientifically based theory to explain the relationship between individual and environment, for Baudelaire's descent into the world of the sordid, or for Flaubert's unrelenting irony. Most directly perhaps, Chénier's epic poems influenced Alfred de Vigny's philosophical works and his subtle orchestration of sounds suggested new possibilities of poetic language to Leconte de Lisle.

Chénier's work during the Revolution transcended the limits of specific literary movements. His last writings not only brought to fruition the fundamental conservatism of the *philosophes* with respect to political matters but exemplified the tradition of humanism in Western civilization. It was paradoxically during the blackest days of his century that his reserves of irony and self-detachment emerged and enabled him at once to extract the universal significance of his experience and become the French Revolution's most eloquent chronicler.

Notes and References

Preface

1. P. A. Chapman et al., *An Anthology of Eighteenth Century French Literature* (Princeton: Princeton University Press, 1930), p. xlii. Wade writes: "The rapid development in the natural sciences, in history, politics, and psychology, during the first half of the century made a general inventory of knowledge imperative. This need became all the more urgent since the century believed implicitly in the solidarity of the sciences and the unity of knowledge. Diversity of thought as well as of method threatened this essential solidarity." Peter Gay, *The Enlightenment, An Interpretation*, vol. I (New York: Alfred A. Knopf, 1966), p. 141: "The philosophes' glorification of criticism and their qualified repudiation of metaphysics make it obvious that the Enlightenment was not an Age of Reason but a Revolt against Rationalism. This revolt took two closely related forms: it rejected the assertion that reason is the sole, or even the dominant, spring of action; and it denied that all mysteries in the world can be penetrated by inquiry."

2. Rémy G. Saisselin, *The Rule of Reason and the Ruses of the Heart* (Cleveland: Case Western Reserve Press, 1970), p. 163: ". . . if the eighteenth century failed generally to produce great or moving poetry, it compensated by producing a great many treatises on poetry in general and odes in particular. . . . Eighteenth century critics and poets wondered about the nature or essence of poetry, its relation to genius and enthusiasm, nature and history, taste and society, and sought to understand why the poetic production of their own times was poor: for it was indeed generally felt that something was wrong." Robert Finch, *The Sixth Sense, Individualism in French Poetry 1686 - 1760* (Toronto: University of Toronto Press, 1966), p. 3: "There is overwhelming evidence that a very large number of people in the eighteenth century cared strongly about poetry." Martin Kopf, *The Poetics of André Chénier* (New York: Columbia University Dissertation, 1972), p. 4. "Since Cartesian rationalism and a scientific spirit of curiosity

regarding all things dominated the age, it was only natural for writers to want to explore the field of aesthetics and to codify their findings in formal treatises."

3. Paul Dimoff, *La Vie et l'oeuvre d'André Chénier jusqu'à la révolution française, 1762 - 1790* (1936; rpt. Geneva: Slatkine, 1970).

4. *Ibid.*, I, p. viii.

5. *Ibid.*, I, p. ix.

6. Clifton Cherpack, "Is There Any Eighteenth-Century French Literature?" *French Review*, 33, No. 1 (1959), 11 - 16; Pierre Chartier, "Le Dix-Huitième Siècle existe-t-il?", *Dix-Huitième Siècle, Revue Annuelle* (1975), 5.

Chapter One

1. Quoted by Dimoff, *Chénier . . . Life*, I, p. 63.

2. Francis Scarfe, *André Chénier, His Life and Work, 1762 - 1794* (Oxford: Oxford University Press, 1965), p. 34; also Francis Scarfe, ed., *André Chénier, Poems* (Oxford: Basil Blackwell, 1961), p. xi.

3. Scarfe, *Poems*, p. ix.

4. Dimoff, *Chénier . . . Life*, vol. I, p. 205.

5. Scarfe, *Poems*, p. x.

Chapter Two

1. Alex Preminger et al., *Princeton Encyclopedia of Poetry and Poetics* (Princeton: Princeton University Press, 1965), p. 636.

2. "Il n'y a pas de bonheur, pour aucune espèce vivante, qu'à suivre ce à quoi la nature la destine." *Essai*, Pléiade, p. 621. Rousseau had written, "L'Homme est né libre, et par-tout il est dans les fers." *Du Contrat Social, Oeuvres complètes*, tome III (Paris: Pléiade, 1964), p. 351.

3. Kopf, p. 24: "His knowledge and veneration of classical antiquity appear on almost every page. . . . But it [his work] is still very much a product of the eighteenth century with its denunciation of clericalism, its emphasis on progress, a free society, and the individuality of the artist."

4. Saisselin, p. 123. Saisselin adds (p. 123): "It is possible . . . to say that part of the confusion in the aesthetics of the eighteenth century came from the mixture of two antithetical systems, one founded upon the concept of nature and the other upon the institution of art: though few, if any, were aware of this confusion, which involved contradictions in thought concerning art, beauty, and nature, and their relation to each other."

5. Daniel Mornet, *French Thought in the Eighteenth Century*, trans. by Lawrence Levin (Hamden, Connecticut: Archon Books, 1969), p. 84.

6. Scarfe, *Chénier . . . Life*, p. 104. In *Les Origines Intellectuelles de la Révolution Française*, 1715 - 1787 (Paris: Armand Colin, 1967) Daniel Mornet wrote that "from 1750 to 1790, the philosophy of disbelief had said nearly everything that it could say. . . . All of France began to *think*. It is a futile speculation to wonder what would have come to France and the Revolution if Montesquieu, Voltaire, Diderot had written nothing. But it seems clear that the movements of opinion, less intense only, less enthusiastic, less rapid, would not have been very different. The great philosophers do not reveal unknown domains . . ." (pp. 469 - 76).

7. Scarfe, *Chénier . . . Life*, p. 105.

8. Margaret Gilman, *The Idea of Poetry in France* (Cambridge: Harvard University Press, 1958), p. 4. Gilman is in general a hostile critic in her discussion of Chénier. Speaking of Chénier's doctrines she states: ". . . one is reminded . . . of the manifestoes of the Pléiade; there is the same intention of restoring poetry to the high place it had occupied in ancient times, of exalting the poet as prophet and interpreter of nature; the same conception of a liberal imitation of the great poets of antiquity. . . . Yet in Chénier's doctrine there is at the same time a belief in emotion as the fountainhead of poetry, a constant plea for naturalness and spontaneity. He never . . . succeeded in reconciling these two conceptions, and this is the chief weakness of his theory as well as of his poetry" (pp. 119 - 120).

9. Dimoff, *Chénier . . . Life*, vol. II, p. 162. Dimoff wrote in the same work (II, pp. 274 - 275): "As a disciple of Montesquieu and Rousseau, Chénier had always affirmed that men of letters could and should use their study, their experience, their memory for the public weal — as valiant as others and more enlightened, to serve the country by the hand and counsel."

10. Scarfe, *Chénier . . . Life*, p. 107.

11. E. B. O. Borgerhoff, *The Freedom of French Classicism* (Princeton: Princeton University Press, 1950), p. 235. Speaking of artists and critics in seventeenth century France, Borgerhoff concludes: ". . . they appreciated the inexplicable in art and the *élan* of the artist. They feared the effect of certain restrictions as much as they agreed on certain principles. They knew the force of hidden beauty and secret charm; they knew the mystery of the sublime. They also knew the reality of instinctive emotional judgments."

12. Louis Bertrand, *La fin du classicisme et le retour à l'antique dans la seconde moitié du xviiie siècle et les premières années du XIXe en France.* (Paris: Librairie Hachette, 1897), p. 31.

13. E. Chaponnière, "L'Esprit Mondain et la poésie lyrique au xviiie siècle," *Revue du Dix-Huitième Siècle*, vol. 2 (1914), 40 - 55.

14. Kopf, pp. 58 - 59.

15. "Elégie," Dimoff, vol. 3, p. 29.

16. R. de Gourmont, "La Philosophie d'André Chénier," *Controverse et le Contemporain*, 2, séries 4 (1883), 673 - 699.

17. E. Estève, "Le sens de la vie dans l'oeuvre d'André Chénier," *Etudes de littérature préromantique* (1923), p. 9.

18. Bertrand, p. 235.

19. C. Kramer, "André Chénier, l'artiste des Bucoliques," *Revue de Hollande*, 3 (1916), 14 - 35.

20. Scarfe, *Chénier* . . . *Life*, p. 111; Kopf, p. 57.

21. Saisselin, p. 109.

22. Estève, p. 16.

23. Dimoff, *Chènier* . . . *Life*, vol. I, p. 320.

24. Charles Maurras, *Oeuvres Capitales*, vol. III (Paris, 1954), pp. 282 - 285.

25. Julian Eugene White, Jr., *Nicolas Boileau* (New York: Twayne, 1969), p. 168.

26. *Ibid.*

27. Emile Faguet, *André Chénier* (Paris: Librairie Hachette, 1902), p. 22.

28. It was while he was staying at Mme de Vercellis' house that Rousseau was taught this precept by the tutor of the Comte de Mellarède's children, the Abbé de Gaime: ". . . si chaque homme pouvait lire dans les coeurs de tous les autres, il y aurait plus de gens qui voudraient descendre que de ceux qui voudraient monter." *Confessions*, Livre Troisième, (Paris: Pléiade, 1959), p. 91.

29. Saisselin, pp. 284 - 285.

30. Clifton Cherpack, "The Structure of Chénier's *L'Invention*," *PMLA*, no. 72 (March, 1957), 74 - 83.

31. Gilman, pp. 119 - 120.

32. Commenting on Chénier's doctrine of creativity, Madeleine Jouglard has observed: "In the *Essai* Chénier distinguished between those who had no plan in writing and those who follow a vast project . . ." "'L'Imitation Inventrice' ou les contradictions d'André Chénier," *Revue de littérature comparée*, VIII (1928), 640 - 653.

33. Emile Faguet, *Histoire de la poésie française de la Renaissance au Romantisme, Vol. X, André Chénier* (Paris: Boivin et Cie., 1936), p. 164. Faguet wrote: "Like Du Bellay and La Fontaine, Chénier means a veritable innutrition by imitation. One must assimilate profoundly the ideas and the phrases borrowed from the ancients and form thus the sugar and the substance of our mind" (p. 164).

34. Saisselin, p. 200.

35. Dimoff, *Chénier . . . Life,* vol. I, pp. 216 - 217: "It is likely that André Chénier's "Epître sur ses ouvrages" was written during the first months of 1787."

36. Kopf, p. 162.

Chapter Three

1. *Princeton Encyclopedia of Poetry and Poetics,* p. 86.

2. Gustave Lanson, *Histoire de la littérature française* (Paris: Librairie Hachette, 1951), p. 850.

3. Yves Le Hir, "La Versification de Chénier dans les 'Bucoliques'," *Information Littéraire,* 6 (1954), 97 - 108.

4. Félix Gaiffe, *Les Bucoliques* (Paris, 1937), p. 65.

5. Anthony Pugh, "On Analyzing Poetry, *La Jeune Tarentine,*" *Modern Languages,* 43 (1962), p. 106.

6. Scarfe, *Chénier . . . Life,* p. 168.

Chapter Four

1. *Princeton Encyclopedia of Poetry and Poetics,* p. 215.

2. Denis de Rougemont, *Love in the Western World* (New York: Harper and Row, 1956), p. 207.

3. Scarfe, *Chénier . . . Life,* p. 28.

4. *Ibid.,* p. 48.

5. Dimoff, *Chénier . . . Life,* vol. I, pp. 161 - 163.

6. Jean Fabre, *Chénier* (Paris: Hatier, 1965), pp. 245 - 246.

7. Pius de Montera, "André Chénier et l'Italie," *Nouvelle Revue d'Italie,* 18 (1921), pp. 121 - 139, 402 - 419.

8. *Princeton Encyclopedia of Poetry and Poetics,* pp. 248 - 249.

Chapter Five

1. Henry Freeman, "Vertu de la Révolution Française: deux jeunes écrivains devant la crise," *Language Quarterly,* XII (Fall-Winter, 1973), pp. 17 - 22.

2. For a more detailed discussion of the American presence in Paris during the two decades before the Revolution see Elizabeth M. Quillen, "L'Idée de Liberté dans la pensée et la poésie d'André Chénier," *Neohelicon,* I, 3 - 4 (1973), 351.

3. Walter, p. 145.
4. *Ibid.*, p. 112.
5. Freeman, p. 17.
6. Scarfe, *Chénier* . . . *Life*, p. 235.
7. *Ibid.*, p. 256.
8. Emile Faguet, *Le Dix-Huitième Siècle; études littéraires* (Paris: Ancienne Librairie Lecène, 1890), pp. 118 - 119.
9. Scarfe, *Chénier* . . . *Life*, p. 237.
10. Freeman, p. 20.
11. Scarfe, *Chénier* . . . *Life*, p. 299.
12. *Ibid.*, p. 300.
13. Vernon Loggins, *André Chénier, His Life, Death and Glory* (Athens, Ohio: Ohio University Press, 1965), p. 214; Scarfe, *Chénier* . . . *Life*, p. 314.
14. Walter, pp. 185 - 186.
15. *Ibid.*, Avant-Propos
16. Lee Harrison, "The Place of André Chénier in Revolutionary Politics," *Queen's Quarterly* (1914), pp. 279 - 293.
17. Mornet, p. 323.

Chapter Six

1. Scarfe, *Chénier* . . . *Life*, p. 304.
2. *Ibid.*, pp. 351 - 352.

Selected Bibliography

BIBLIOGRAPHICAL MATERIAL

GLACHANT, PAUL. *André Chénier, critique et critiqué.* Paris: Alphonse
  Lemerre, 1902. A valuable tool for surveying nineteenth century editions and criticism of Chénier's work. Dimoff's *La Vie et l'oeuvre
  d'André Chénier des origines jusqu'à la révolution française* contains
  a lengthy bibliography of such items as libraries and public archives
  relating to Chénier; a listing of the manuscripts and editions of all
  primary sources; works relating to Chénier's origins, ancestors, and
  family; bibliographical works, sources of Chénier's works and influences; general literary studies; and a section of works dealing with
  language, style, and versification.

PRIMARY SOURCES

DIMOFF, PAUL. ed. *Oeuvres complètes d'André Chénier.* 3 vols. Paris:
  Delagrave, I. Bucoliques, 1908; II. Poèmes, Hymnes, Théâtre, 1910;
  III, Elégies, Epîtres, Odes, Iambes, 1912. Numerous reeditions have
  appeared since 1919. This edition offers many useful thematic groupings of Chénier's poems, particularly of the bucolics. Obviously the ti-
  tle is a misnomer inasmuch as the writings from 1790 to 1794 are not
  included.
CHÉNIER, ANDRÉ. "L'Invention" — avec introduction et notes par Paul
  Dimoff. Paris: Librairie Nizet, 1966. This edition is a model of pains-
  taking scholarship. In addition to an authoritative version of
  "L'Invention" and a long introduction, it contains drafts of the poem
  and 134 pages of detailed notes.
André Chénier, Poems. Selected and edited by Francis Scarfe. Oxford: Basil
  Blackwell, 1961. An anthology containing seventy-five representative
  poems with short notes and a good brief introduction to Chénier.
  Scarfe has included passages from longer works such as "L'Hermès,"
  "L'Amérique," and "La République des Lettres."

159

André Chénier. Oeuvres complètes, première édition intégrale. ed. by
Gérard Walter. Paris: Bibliothèque de la Pléiade, 1958. This volume is
particularly useful as a source of Chénier's political writings. Some of
Walter's groupings, notably the love poems and the bucolics, and distinctions he makes between finished and unfinished verse, are inconsistent. This volume is nonetheless essential because it contains a
detailed chronological listing from 1819 to 1957 of all editions of Chénier's poetry and prose and studies of his works. A glossary of all
mythological names found in Chénier is also very useful.

SECONDARY SOURCES

D'Aubarède, Gabriel. *André Chénier.* Paris: Hachette, 1970. Reasonably
informative. Occasionally reads like a novel. Contains not very rele-
vant literary-historical material.

Dimoff, Paul. *La Vie et l'oeuvre d'André Chénier des origines jusqu'à la
révolution française, 1762 - 1790.* 2 vols. Paris: Librairie E. Droz,
1936. Geneva: Slatkine Reprints, 1970. These two volumes reveal
Dimoff's vast erudition and are invaluable as reference guides. They
are ponderous, however, and, being almost exclusively devoted to
Chénier's intellectual development, present a one-sided picture in
which Chénier's vitality is often totally obscured. Moreover, as I have
stated in my Introduction, I take issue with Dimoff's contention that
Chénier led two distinct existences, the one literary and the other
political.

Cherpack, Clifton. "The Structure of Chénier's *L'Invention.*" *PMLA*, no.
72 (March, 1957), 74 - 183. One of the best articles on "L'Invention."
Shows its contradictions and tensions. Argues that despite its
doctrinaire message, the poem should be treated as a work of
literature and discussed in terms of poetic principles.

Estève, E. "Le sens de la vie dans l'oeuvre d'André Chénier." In *Etudes de
littérature préromantique*, pp. 1 - 137. Paris: Champion, 1923. A fine
essay. Author concludes that Chénier, "born into the confines of two
glorious literary epochs, doesn't belong to either one exclusively, that
he was in literature what he was in life, an independent and isolated
figure."

Fabre, Jean. *André Chénier.* Connaissance des lettres. Paris: Hachette,
1965. One of the best introductions to Chénier. Insightful comments
on the bucolics and elegies. An intelligent, readable study.

Faguet, Emile. *André Chénier.* Paris: Hachette, 1902. A pioneering study
with respect to analysis of Chénier's evolution in subject matter and
style. Faguet distinguishes Chénier's *première matière* (the desire to
incorporate the soul of the ancients in his work), his *seconde matière*
(Chénier's worldly Paris period), and his *troisième matière* ("his

profoundly personal accent"). Although Faguet is considered out-
moded by certain critics he remains an important figure in Chénier
studies.

————. *Histoire de la poésie française de la Renaissance au Romantisme.*
Vol. X. *André Chénier.* Paris: Boivin et Cie., 1936. Traces in greater
detail than the 1902 study the main currents of Chénier's thought.
Concludes that Chénier is France's greatest elegiac poet.

FREEMAN, HENRY. "Vertu de la Révolution Française: deux écrivains devant
la crise." *Language Quarterly,* XII (Fall-Winter, 1973), 17 - 22.
Discussion of impact of Revolution on Chénier and Chateaubriand.
Author manages to present a clearer picture of Chenier's political
philosophy in a few pages than La Vallée does in an entire book.

GAIFFE, FÉLIX. *Les Bucoliques.* Paris: Cours de Sorbonne, 1937. An important study on the sources of many of Chénier's bucolics. Useful
material on the rising interest in antiquity in the latter half of the
eighteenth century.

DE GOURMONT, RÉMY, "La Philosophie d'André Chénier." *Controverse et le
Contemporain,* 2, série 4 (1883), 673 - 699. One of the first pieces of
criticism to attempt a general assessment of Chénier's thought. Some
of Gourmont's conclusions appear naïve today. Some psychological
insights.

HARASZTI, JULES. *La Poésie d'André Chénier.* Paris: Hachette, 1892. A
polemical work. Haraszti is unsympathetic of Chénier. Concludes
that Chénier's art is marred by excessive imitation and that much of
his work can be labelled archeological poetry.

HERBILLON, CNEL. *André Chénier.* Paris: Tallandier, 1949. An uninspired
study. Not very readable because of the number of quotations.

JOUGLARD, MADELEINE. "L'Imitation Inventrice ou les Contradictions
d'André Chénier." *Revue de littérature comparée,* VIII (1928), 640 -
653. An interesting article which amplifies Faguet's theory of *innutrition.*

KOPF, MARTIN. "The Poetics of André Chénier." Columbia University,
University Microfilms, 1972. One of the best studies to emerge on
Chénier in recent years. An essential work for the layman and scholar
alike. Kopf discusses with insight and clarity the state of poetry in
eighteenth-century France and Chénier's views on art and the artist,
as revealed in five works.

KRAMER, C. "André Chénier, l'artiste des Bucoliques." *Revue de Hollande,*
3 (1916), 14 - 34. Rather ethereal article in which such terms as
beauty, taste, and order in the bucolics are discussed without being
clearly defined.

————. *André Chénier et la poésie parnassienne: Leconte de Lisle.* Paris:
Librairie Ancienne Honoré Champion, 1925. Chiefly interesting in its
discussion of Leconte de Lisle's transformations of Chénier's themes
and language.

————. "Les Poèmes Epiques d'André Chénier." *Neophilologus* (1920 - 1921) V: 210 - 218, 298 - 309; VI: 13 - 28, 149 - 141. "L'Hermès," "L'Amérique," "Suzanne." Excellent study of the background of these three works combined with detailed textual analysis.

LA VALLÉE, O. *André Chénier et les Jacobins.* Paris: Calmann-Lévy, 1881. A ponderous study. Marred by being too descriptive. Author's point of view is not always clear.

LE HIR, YVES. "La Qualification dans les 'Bucoliques' d'André Chénier." *Français Moderne,* 22 (1954), 97 - 106.

————. "La Versification de Chénier dans les 'Bucoliques.' " *Information Littéraire,* 6 (1954), 97 - 108.

————. "L'expression du ,sentiment amoureux dans l'oeuvre d'André Chénier." *Les Lettres Romanes* (1955). Three interesting studies by Le Hir that give detailed analyses of Chénier's use of language.

LOGGINS, VERNON. *André Chénier, His Life, Death and Glory.* Athens, Ohio: Ohio University Press, 1965. A somewhat melodramatic treatment of Chénier that offers little new information.

MASSON, PIERRE-MAURICE. "L'Influence d'André Chénier sur Alfred de Vigny." *Revue d'Histoire Littéraire de la France* (January-March, 1909), 1 - 48. Traces history of literary battles involving Chénier's contribution to the Romantics. Concludes that Vigny was influenced by Chénier but retained much originality.

DE MONTERA, PIUS. "André Chénier et l'Italie." *Nouvelle Revue d'Italie,* 18 (1921), 121 - 139, 402, 419. A well-written article. Traces the origins of Chénier's attraction for Italy and how this sentiment was expressed in his elegies.

MORILLOT, PAUL. *André Chénier.* Paris: Lecène, Oudin et Cie., 1894. An interesting study. Morillot concludes that Chénier's reputation will rest on his *iambes.*

POIROT, JEAN. "La Théorie de la Création Poétique chez André Chénier et chez les Romantiques." *Neuphilologische Mitteilungen* (November-December, 1900), 1 - 13. Interpretation of Chénier's theory of poetic creation. Valuable because Poirot underscores distinctions between Chénier and Romantics.

QUILLEN, ELISABETH M. "L'Idée de Liberté dans la pensée et la poésie d'André Chénier." *Neohelicon,* I, 3 - 4 (1973), 351 - 363. Well-written article. Sets Chénier's political theory against the background of the Enlightenment; concludes that the concept of liberty was foremost in Chénier's thought long before the outbreak of the Revolution.

SCARFE, FRANCIS. *André Chénier, His Life and Work, 1762 - 1794.* Oxford: The Clarendon Press, 1965. The best general introduction to Chénier. Author concludes that Chénier represents a vital element in European tradition because of his efforts to keep the past alive. One minor criticism: Scarfe's style is sometimes too flamboyant.

VENZAC, G. *Jeux d'Ombre et de Lumière sur la Jeunesse d'André Chénier.* Paris: Gallimard, 1957. Claims to find proof of deep religious sentiment in Chénier. Written by a clergyman who taught at L'Institut Catholique. An unconvincing, ponderous work.

VIANEY, JOSEPH. "Les Poésies antiques d'André Chénier et l'épopée contemporaine." *Revue des Lettres Françaises et Etrangères* (October, 1899), pp. 249 - 264. Examines relationship between Chénier's epic poems and contemporary attitudes toward the genre.

WALTER, GÉRARD. *André Chénier, Son Milieu et Son Temps.* Paris: Robert Lafont, 1947. A highly controversial work. Walter, in strong opposition to Chénier's politics, writes that Chénier's countrymen recognized that he was a dangerous polemicist and that it "was a dangerous political enemy" who was sent to the guillotine. Faced with two choices, that of committing himself to the Revolution or avoiding the struggle, Chénier clearly indicated the path he intended to follow.

ZYRONSKI, E. "L'Humanisme de Chénier et son poème sur L'Invention." *Revue des Lettres Françaises et Étrangères,* I (1899). A provocative article whose conclusions are debatable. Sees "L'Invention" as a manifesto against humanism. Feels Chénier reveals himself as opposed to the method of the humanists, which supposes that the domain of poetry has been entirely exhausted by the ancients.

BACKGROUND STUDIES

BERTRAND, L. *La fin du classicisme et le retour à l'antique dans la seconde moitié du xviiie siècle et les premières années du XIXe en France.* Paris: Hachette, 1897. Discussing the many unfinished portions of Chénier's work, Bertrand contends that Chénier had an uncritical admiration for the Ancients and that there is a stérile quality in his work.

CHAPONNIÈRE, E. "L'Esprit Mondain et la poésie lyrique au xviiie siècle." *Revue du Dix-Huitième Siècle,* vol. 2 (1914). An excellent study. The best introduction to the social factors that influenced poetry in eighteenth century France.

GAY, PETER. *The Enlightenment: An Interpretation.* I. *The Rise of Modern Paganism.* New York: Alfred A. Knopf, 1966, II. *The Science of Freedom.* New York: Alfred A. Knopf, 1969. A classic; indispensable for an understanding of the Enlightenment.

GILMAN, MARGARET. *The Idea of Poetry in France. From Houdar de la Motte to Baudelaire.* Cambridge: Harvard University Press, 1958. Useful as an introduction to the aesthetic theories held by the major writers in eighteenth century France. Less reliable in its treatment of Chénier and the Romantics.

LEFEBVRE, GEORGES. *The French Revolution.* 2 vols. Translated by Elizabeth Moss Evanson. New York: Columbia University Press,

1962. Still remains the best single work on the Revolution. Volume two contains an extensive bibliography.

MORNET, DANIEL. *French Thought in the Eighteenth Century.* Translated by Lawrence Levin. Hamden Connecticut: Archon Books, 1969. Considered a classic. A fine cohesive study of the major intellectual, social, and religious currents in France during the Enlightenment.

POTEZ, HENRI. *L'Elégie en France avant le Romantisme.* Paris: Calmann-Lévy, 1897. Rigorous examination of the genre with a large section devoted to its origins. A long chapter on Chénier. Study would have been improved by an indication of the author's sources, which are not always obvious.

SAISSELIN, RÉMY G. *The Rule of Reason and the Ruses of the Heart: A Philosophical Dictionary of Classical French Criticism, Critics, and Aesthetic Issues.* Cleveland: The Press of Case Western Reserve University, 1970. An indispensable and often brilliant study of the terms used in poetics and aesthetic theory during the seventeenth and eighteenth centuries in France. This book is a model of painstaking scholarship combined with wit and style.

STAVAN, HENRY A. "Le lyrisme dans la Poésie Française, 1760 - 1820, critiques justes et injustes." *Revue des sciences humaines,* 149 (1973), 85 - 93. An interesting article. Traces evolution of critical attitudes toward eighteenth century French poetry. Stavan concludes that lyricism in the last forty years of the century was more impersonal than in the first half ("it is the art of the group rather than that of the individual"), yet it was this lyricism that prepared the way for Romanticism after 1820.

WADE, IRA O. *The Intellectual Origins of the French Enlightenment.* Princeton: Princeton University Press, 1972. A brilliant, encyclopedic study.

Index